One Degree Beyond:
A Reiki Journey Into
Energy Medicine

Second Edition

Your 21-Day Step-By-Step Guide to Relax, Open and Celebrate...

ONE
DEGREE
BEYOND
2ND EDITION

*A Reiki
Journey
Into
Energy
Medicine*

JANEANNE NARRIN

"What magic can manifest itself when one dares to explore beyond the usual and the apparent?"

This book is manufactured in the United States of America.
Cover art by Nichole Parsons
Book design by Walker-Blessing

Published by Little White Buffalo Publishing Cottage
12345 Lake City Way N.E., Suite 204
Seattle, Washington 98125
http://www.littlewhitebuffalo.com

Publisher's Cataloging-in-Publication
(Provided by Quality Books, Inc.)

Narrin, Janeanne.
    One degree beyond : a Reiki journey into energy medicine/
    Janeanne Narrin. — 2nd ed.
    p. cm.
    Includes bibliographical references and index.
    ISBN: 0-9658545-4-X

    1. Reiki (Healing system) 2. Stress management. 3.
    Relaxation. 4. Alternative medicine. I. Title

RZ403.R45N37 1998   615.8'52
                         QBI98-324

10 9 8 7 6 5 4 3

THIS BOOK IS PRINTED ON
RECYCLED PAPER

"Just trust life:
Life will bring you high,
If only you are careful in selecting
In the maze of events,
Those influences or those paths
Which can bring you each time
A little more upward.

Life has to be discovered
And built step by step
A great charm..."

Pierre Teilhard de Chardin

Contents

PART ONE: EXPLORATION

Chapter 1: Relax, Open, Celebrate

Chapter 2: Fortuitous Detours...Change and Innovation

PART TWO: APPLICATION

APPENDICES

Appendix A: Making Contact

Appendix B: Complementary Systems

Appendix C: Resources

Index

FOREWORD
By Paula Horan, Ph.D.

Janeanne Narrin's long career in personnel psychology has provided her with extensive insight into the causes of and possible solutions to stress, anxiety, and alienation in the present day work place. With broad experience in management and employee development systems, she is skilled in the ways of the business world. She is also a gifted painter and poet and thus is able to bring into her perspective the silent, healing, meditative state of the artist. The pages that follow are a joy to experience as she draws you in with her incredible ability to "talk story" and wax poetic in her own unique style. She has the gift of being able to address the high-powered, left-brained, *type-a personality,* opening him or her to the possibilities of the peaceful state of silent "beingness" which Reiki evokes. This is in sharp contrast to the state most people normally experience (whether left- or right-brained), which is limited to the "doer" or ego-centered consciousness from which most of the world is still suffering and trying desperately (albeit unconsciously) to move beyond.

Janeanne opens a door for the reader to go deeper into the process of Reiki than is possible in most other books. Having practiced Reiki for several years before moving into her mastership, she is well grounded in her perception of and connection to Universal Reiki and, in **One Degree Beyond**, fully demonstrates her ability to convey its essence. Indeed, her *gift* as a healer and teacher enable her to "demystify" Reiki without taking the mystery out of it!

Janeanne points the way to the direct experience of Reiki clearly, as she helps the reader towards an awareness that Reiki, as pure heart energy, is beyond mind and cannot be "understood." Reiki can be perceived through the "vision" of the heart; and heart knowledge is perceived through the transference and open reception of love. Reiki, as Universal Life Force Energy, is the very energy of Heart. When used consciously, it can put us in touch with deeper understandings. Without words, it can allow us to relax and to enjoy the unlimited potential that we are.

For the uninitiated, Reiki is rapidly becoming a global phenomenon. Both traditional and non-traditional practitioners are coming to recognize its many benefits. Even some insurance companies are now considering giving remuneration for Reiki treatments. Janeanne Narrin's special emphasis on Reiki's long and short term benefits, when used to counterbalance illness, stress, anxiety, and alienation in the modern world, may further promote its popularity as a healing tool and as a means to the development of an alternative approach to preventative self-care. More importantly, however, she demonstrates that Reiki is connected to a changing worldview, one which emphasizes harmony and inner connectedness in nature. She challenges her readers to take that extra step, to move beyond outmoded egocentric thinking to a place of both self-realization and global responsibility.

Paula Horan, Ph.D.
author of *Empowerment Through Reiki*
and *Abundance Through Reiki*

ACKNOWLEDGMENTS

No book is the work of a single individual, and I wish to acknowledge and to thank the many teachers, past and present, who have contributed so much to my own understanding of the process of self-discovery and empowerment.

Special appreciation to the following people whose wise words and insights are included in this book: Pat and Bob Green, Tonie and C.B., Nancy Schneider, David and Bonnyrae, Maliki, Ann, Jean, Thrinley, Bruce and Jen, Chris and Steve, Rob and Helen, Nancy, Joan, Tracy and Tom, Christi, Cherie, Jerry, Andrea, Norman and Lynn, Heidemarie, Nichole and Randy, Therese, Charlie and Cleo, Wendi, Fred Boyd, Garreth, Mary and Carolyn, Tom and Faye, Cathy and Steve, Jim and Michelle, Hazel, Russ, Regina, Judy, John, and Scott.

Bless you, Joan Marie, wherever you are.

To my mentors in the corporate world, Judy Bankey, Donna Censoni, Louise DePutron, John Goldsworthy, John Hale, Jim Hanje, Andy Hasley, Hank Hamilton, John and Nancy Kufchock, Sam Mancuso, Mike Mikolay, Tom Moylan, Terry Murphy, Tony Raubolt, Steve Sicotte-Kelly, Scott Symons and Bernie Wesol, three grateful bows. Norm, thanks for the "Smirbs."

Thanks to Reiki Master Paula Horan, Ph.D., Reiki Masters Wanja Twan, Rick Bockner, Earlene Gleisner, Mari Hall, Amy Rowland, and Douglas Morris and the "Reiki Friends," Norma Jean Young, Becky Farrar-Koch and Jo Angelina for their support, and to Phyllis Lei Furumoto for just *being* who you are. To my students, who have shared their wisdom with me, thanks for your encouragement.

Applause to those who took time to read and reread the manuscript, and offer editorial comment—to John Boylan, Mike, Jo, David, Karen and Jeremy, John, Carol Wright, and to my best critic and friend, Steve. Special thanks to Lauren, and to Ann Elniff, and Faye Kendall whose dedication and word processing skills were invaluable. Megasmiles and appreciation to Art Walker for his invaluable contributions to the book design.

To Lara Lavi, The Poet Schrecengost, Lee Henderson and Wind-in-the-Feather, whose poetry speaks to me, thank you.

To King James the Cat, who often sat upon the manuscript, imbuing it with the happy energy of resonant Maine Coon purrs, and to dear Goldendog, Maggie, there from the start, my warmest appreciation.

Finally, special thanks to my father, Edward Aloysius O'Donnell, for his steadfast interest in this book, and to my son, John Thomas Narrin, for his way of saying just the right thing at just the right time.

*J*NTRODUCTION

Every life has at its core a potential that quietly and unobtrusively asks to be fulfilled. It is an important part of the original blessing of being in this world. "Purpose" is one word for this potential; "dream" is another. Sometimes, our potential is apparent and "out there"— a specific dream, a strong goal or set of goals. In some individuals, however, that awareness of life's purpose lies dormant, hidden behind what psychologists like to call our "subconscious plane." There are, of course, many ways of tapping into one's life potential and making it a reality. This book is about one significant way, Reiki, the artscience of healing. Regardless of where you are in terms of being aware of and actualizing your special dream, *One Degree Beyond* can assist this process. Readers can expect to become familiar with, learn about, and have opportunities to actually come in contact with Reiki healing practices. No one can predict exactly where new knowledge and experience will take them. So it is that I also will not predict what you will learn or experience from your involvement with this book. What I will say is that being open minded and receptive to the concepts and exercises in the book can pay huge dividends in terms of assisting you to connect with your life's purpose and to discover very useful approaches to better health.

One of the major themes of *One Degree Beyond* is learning to tap into and engage the processes for our personal growth and development. A second significant emphasis in the book is connected to the first. Woven into the formula for advancing our individual well-being is a need for recognizing our place in and supporting the global community, for bringing our human endeavors into alignment with a *partnership* model of reality. In this model, everybody wins, everyone's actions contribute to the highest good of all concerned. In their prayers, Native Americans refer to this extended sense of community as "all of our relations." All of our "relations" of the global community consists not only of our fellow human beings, but also the animals, plants, minerals, the rocks, mountains and seas, the deserts, swamps and wetlands, the great plains and wild forests. We are also specially connected to the abundant creative energy which is associated with discovery and accomplishment within the human community.

This *ecocentric* viewpoint can be directly opposed to the traditional and prevailing *egocentric* worldview. The latter perspective places man at the center of the universe and has all of the other elements and forces of nature at his service and bidding. The clear results of this worldview are quite frequently disastrous not only for other elements of nature, but for humankind. The destruction of our rainforests, acid rain, smog, the extinction of certain animals, and the more recent concerns about changing weather patterns associated with *El Niño* are a few examples where the separation of the apparent interests of humankind from the interests of the rest of nature has endangered the human species. One hardly needs to mention the more direct destruction associated with war. An ecocentric world perspective, on the other hand, constitutes a recognition of the fact that all of the elements and forces of nature are mutually dependent. It aims at harmony and cooperation, not destruction and the endangering of all species.

Fully understanding the notion that we are connected to and interdependent upon all of the other living and active elements within the global community has some significant implications in terms of how we live and act in the world. Recognizing our interconnectedness and our interdependence, it is important above all that we act in ways that will preserve and nurture whatever is positive and promotes harmony in the world, that we do whatever we can to support the global community.

How can we do this effectively? One obvious way is to continue the current pattern of enacting and enforcing laws aimed at protecting the natural universe. We live, at least theoretically, in a "civilized" world, one where nations and peoples are governed by the rule of law. There is no question that legislation and rules and regulations can and do help. So we continue this approach. Unfortunately, and all too obviously however, the rule of human law is frequently contradictory, arbitrary, difficult to enforce, and easy to manipulate and ignore. In other words, human laws are in large measure woefully inadequate to the task and in some instances actually widen the gap between humankind and the rest of the natural world. It could even be argued that the necessity for human laws is evidence of the extent to which we are separated from and even are unaware of natural law.

However much the protective and nature-honoring laws projected and developed by societies may help in preserving our natural world, the benefit of "all of our relations" is not really something that can be decreed from the outside.

There is a logic and an order to nature, especially as it relates to the harmonious coexistence of all of its forces and elements. Above all, nature is *process*; all living things are part of that process. A clear understanding of that process and our relationship to it is the first step in getting tuned into natural law, into what is right for ourselves and for our world. What is revealed to anyone who is truly receptive to the messages of natural law, is that all of nature is involved in a deep healing partnership process. There exists an empathic resonance between healer and "healee," between nature and humankind.

So clearly, more than societal law is required if we are to realize and derive full benefits from this partnership. We need to find new approaches and ways of looking at (or rediscover old approaches and old ways of looking at) the issue of how to support and restructure our global community. The approach emphasized in *One Degree Beyond* begins at home, with ourselves, with our personal integrity, and with our own energy. In other words, we have to become ourselves, whole and healthy individuals. We have to think for ourselves, wean ourselves away from unhealthy and negative outside influence, take good care of ourselves emotionally and physically, and find and begin following our purpose in life. And we have to be open and intuitively grasp the particular strands of universal law that apply in a given situation.

In the energetic model of reality there is no separation. Focusing upon our own wholehearted well-being, letting it flow through our lives and out to others, like a rippling effect, will eventually help manifest a wholesome and healthy global community.

There are many different tools for such a transformation. *One Degree Beyond* presents Reiki, the practice of the ancient art of whole systems healing, and boldly proposes that we are dual citizens of both the energetic and physical realms. Not only do we have bodies and minds, but we also partake in and embody the very energies that create the universe—and this in our perception, moment by moment anew. Reiki practitioners discover that *energy is a most precious resource and can be directly touched.*

Not too many years ago, the parable of the "100th monkey" was widely popular and often quoted. It went like this: if, one by one, a hundred monkeys on a distant island learn how to use sticks for picking bananas, the knowledge of picking bananas with sticks all of a sudden becomes an integral part of monkey consciousness. All monkeys everywhere around the world will then be privy to this knowledge and be able to use sticks to that end.

The principle of a vanguard few preparing a shift in consciousness applies to humankind as well, and has inspired many changes in our history. Understanding this, Reiki practitioners do not see Reiki as a sophisticated and blissfully esoteric pacifier for the individuals who choose endlessly to wallow in their woundedness. Nor do we see Reiki merely as a solace for people in need, though it is frequently that. Rather, we know it to be *energy, a powerful, positive life-force* that is accessible to those who are receptive, and who will train themselves to become agents of change. These willing and trained agents of change can contribute to a desperately needed shift in individual consciousness and ultimately help refresh and preserve our global community. *Anyone* can be such an agent. However, the more dedicated one is to what one is doing, the more focused one is on identifying, activating, and achieving one's own potential, the more impact one will have as an agent of change.

Generally, Reiki is described as a gentle hands-on technique of energy exchange rediscovered a little over a century ago in Meiji-era Japan by Dr. Mikao Usui, and transmitted to the present day through an unbroken line of successors and practitioners. Quite a few books have been published on Reiki in this vein, a number of which are cited in this book and listed in Appendix C: Resources. **One Degree Beyond** honors that tradition, the notion of an ancient art of healing rediscovered. However, it is also important to see Reiki as being on the cutting edge of both contemporary science and modern spiritual inquiry. Anyone familiar with the work of David Bohm, Fritjof Capra, Gary Zukav, F. David Peat, or Rupert Sheldrake, for example, or the thought of J. Krishnamurti, Matthew Fox, Thomas Merton, Thomas Berry, and especially Pierre Teilhard de Chardin will find compatibility, a resonance, in the theory and practices of Reiki.

If the practice of Reiki is to become the truly transformative experience that it can be, it is necessary to avoid the trap of interpreting this experience from the perspective of outmoded beliefs and models of thinking which rely on a subject/object polarity. Such a focus totally obscures the field within which the dance of subject and object unfolds in the first place. By blotting out the field, we deprive ourselves of its nourishing qualities. The force, then, cannot be with us.

To counteract our proclivity for heroically remaining stuck in the same old rut of reductionist distortions, *One Degree Beyond* (as in one degree beyond the apparent choices of outmoded thinking) elucidates the very practical and applicable relationship between Reiki and modern scientific and spiritual thinking and uses the tools of self-inquiry to open new doors of perception.

How To Use This Book

For those readers already familiar with Reiki and to those who are already receptive to the notion of energy healing, welcome and enjoy.

For those readers who have reservations: it is not necessary that you as reader agree with and subscribe wholeheartedly to the ideas and practical applications outlined in *One Degree Beyond* in order to derive benefits. In fact, some of you may already doubt, disagree with, or have strong reservations about many of the underlying assumptions associated with the phenomenon of energy medicine. This book is not intended to challenge your beliefs, to argue or reason you to some particular point of view.

My advice to you is *try*. Try to read with as open a mind as you can. Try to do some of the exercises. Above all, do what you can to be open to *process* and to experience without labeling and attempting to intellectually define. Just for the moments of your journey with this book, suspend your disbelief. And later, if you still have doubts, disagreements, and concerns, then express them and let them come out.

My guess is that *One Degree Beyond* will prove valuable to you to the extent that you are able to simply *be* with it. My best wishes are extended to you on your journey.

part one: exploration

1

Relax, Open, Celebrate...

"Grandfather, Sacred One, teach us love, compassion, honor, that we may heal the Earth and heal each other."

Ojibwe Prayer

Imagine

Imagine walking barefoot on a path of fragrant bark...
feeling the summer sun on your head, and the warmth on your feet...
reaching down with your hands...
extending, to touch that bark...
holding shape, form, texture...
and knowing, in a way you have never
known before.

Imagine, as you walk on,
and, as the path opens out into yellow sunlight,
giving way under foot to sweet, green grass,
that you pause to look about.

There, within sight, lies a grove
whose tender blossoms grace this day, and
a golden hammock
suspended 'neath the trees
sways
to beckon you.

Oh, how your very being vibrates with this pulsing place...
and, now, from the hammock
suspended 'neath those trees
suspended in space,
suspended in time,

You own the moment...
feel whole,
at peace,
Imagine.

Wind-in-the-Feather

"The voyage of discovery lies not in finding new landscapes,
but in having new eyes."

~ Marcel Proust

State of the World Address: Stress, Anxiety, and Alienation - Signals to an Endangered Planet

"*A*ll is well,"enthused the 18th Century English poet, Robert Burns, in his mid-century report, *Essay on Man.* The worldview implied in this assertion reflected the age in which it was written, the so-called "Age of Optimism." It was a time, in England at least and for the upper class, when things did seem to be all right. Intellectual historians are fond of the term "The Enlightenment" to describe an era of unbridled confidence in the powers of the human mind and human ingenuity to answer all the great riddles of existence and to discover God's "natural laws." Philosophers, scientists (often one and the same), politicians, even artists were confident that they could achieve perfection in all areas of life. But this was illusion. For all of its splendors and intellectual optimism, the 18th Century in Europe was also a time of incessant wars, revolutions, droughts, famine, and severe economic depressions. It was a time of chaos, confusion, skepticism, anxiety, and stress.

"He who knows Self as the enjoyer of the honey from the flowers of the senses ever-present within, ruler of time, goes beyond fear."

Upanishads
800 B.C.

Hasn't it always been so? Hasn't there always been such a dichotomy, going all the way back to the days of the early hunter-gatherers—aspects of existence which seem good and positive and aspects of existence which are negative and stressful, times when everything seemed clear, structured, and logical and times when doubt and chaos reigned supreme? Can one world even exist without the other?

I don't know what term should be used to accurately describe 18th Century Europe. Perhaps there is no such term. As I look at my time, this time, this 20th Century nearing its end, is there any term, or simple set of descriptive terms, which can capture its essence? I doubt it. What can be said is that we live in a time of great achievement and innovation, a time of technical and scientific advances, of discoveries and new approaches to the diagnosis and treatment of illness, of faster and more accessible modes of transportation, of spectacular innovations in communications and entertainment technology, and of the development of numerous modern "conveniences" to lighten our tasks. (Of course, these things are true for only some people, in some places, some of the time.) In the global arena, in addition to some of the advances just noted, it is possible to argue that this is a time when the prospects of global conflict (a world war) and consequently the use of nuclear weapons to resolve conflicts are greatly diminished. The list of positive accomplishments and improvements is almost inexhaustible.

Just as obviously, we live in a time of considerable and constant anxiety and stress, a time when humankind has alienated itself from its natural allies. There is no shortage of observers ready and willing to point out the negative and self- destructive forces at work in contemporary life. Some of these commentators have suggested that for every technological advance, there is a corresponding increase in stress and anxiety. It seems difficult to argue with them if we look at the many so-called "advances" in modern, "sophisticated" medicine, for example. We have become pill pushers. We have extended the life span of people, but we have not kept pace and developed the means to make these longer lives comfortable and worth living. We have created a system of treating and caring for people which often feels cold, dependent, and depressing.

Other observers have suggested that in human affairs, progress is not a straight linear process, not a matter of constant upward movement, and definitely not predictable. Rather, some argue that progress seems to move in an elliptical pattern, with ups and downs, and hopefully a gradual improvement. Certainly much of economic theory would fit this pattern.

Still others point to the clear negative evidences of modern discoveries and accomplishments, note that the 20th Century has seen the development (and use) of nuclear weapons, increasingly experiences the destruction of our rain forests, the air we breathe, the protective ozone layer, and our waters. This "century of progress" has witnessed two major world wars and numerous other armed conflicts where the most technically advanced weapons have rained destruction on peoples and the natural environment. And finally there are the observers of time movement, who note that the pace of modern living is moving at such a bewildering speed that valued customs and traditions and ways of interacting are being sacrificed and often lost entirely, bringing in their wake confusion, doubt, anger, and alienation. The "buzz" list of modern ills is also nearly inexhaustible.

Undoubtedly, there are at least as many ways of looking at our current world, and especially our own personal situation, as there are people in the world. On the surface, in the appearance of things, there seems to be this duality—some things, some lives, or moments in lives, are "good"; some things, some lives, or moments in lives, are "bad." However, I want to suggest to you that this is an illusion. It is not simply a

"One of the most damaging consequences of looking to the world to satisfy our inner needs is a competitive mode of consciousness.... It promotes blinkered thinking and shortsightedness."

Peter Russell
The White Hole inTime

case of choosing between "the glass is half-full" and "the glass is half-empty." These apparently competing world perspectives are really not in competition. They are actually compatible and complementary. The truth is that the glass is both half-full and half-empty. However, when we are euphoric or happy, we will tend to see the world from a half-full perspective. Just as when we are confused and stressed, anxious or depressed, our tendency will be to see the glass as at best half-empty. Very obviously, these are states of mind; they do not describe reality, merely a view of reality. I do not mean to suggest that the negative elements in our lives and in our universe are untrue or an illusion. Surely they exist, and *One Degree Beyond* is at least partially an attempt to explain, demonstrate, and engage readers in an approach to help deal with them. But they do not exist alone, they exist in relationship, a relationship to all other elements and energies, they are part of a continuum, parts of the whole.

An Emerging Understanding

*D*on't look now, but something significant is going on in terms of our understanding of the universe and our place in it. Our times are witnessing a major shift in the way scientists, mathematicians, economists, artists, medical researchers, social activists, management theorists, educators, and technology innovators look at the universe. This shift in consciousness, based partially on new approaches to science, has implications for all of us. The old Newtonian worldview has undergone an onslaught, first from the theorists who advanced the notion of relativity (where the linear approach to time and space was challenged), then from the advocates of quantum mechanical physics (where exact measurement came into question), and most recently from what a growing number of commentators are calling the new science of "chaos theory."

"… the opportunity of our time is to integrate science's understanding of the universe with more ancient intuitions concerning the meaning and destiny of the human. The promise of this work is that through such an enterprise, the human species as a whole will begin to embrace a common meaning and a coherent program of action…."

Brian Swimme, Ph.D.
The Hidden Heart of the Cosmos

Without going too far into chaos theory, which we could call "an awakening," the key ideas for our purposes are:

• The universe can no longer fully be understood from the perspective of orderly, logical patterns and from an approach to science which emphasizes only particularized research.

• Chaos and disorder coexist in the world with, and have a connection to, order and structure.

• Patterns of behavior and order are not things imposed from without, do not exist as external truths. Rather, they are organic, they come from within, from out of chaos.

• It becomes extremely difficult to predict behavior in a world which does not repeat itself, which is organic, dynamic, and interconnected but not linear.

• Nevertheless, by looking at whole systems and by seeing the universe as one whole, interacting, interconnected, interrelated, organic energy system in which whatever affects the one element has the potential to affect the whole, it is possible to bring new knowledge and new insights to the process of understanding our world, its origins, operating principles, and direction.

"Hail ye sweet courtesies of life,
for smooth do ye make the road of it!
Like grace and beauty which beget
inclinitions to love at first sight:
'tis ye who open this door and let
the stranger in."

Laurence Sterne
A Sentimental Journey through France and Italy

Why Talk About This?

"What is demanded of us now is to change attitudes that are so deeply bound into our basic cultural patterns that they seem to us as an imperative of the very nature of our being, a dictate of our genetic coding as a species. In clinical language, we are in a deep cultural pathology. We can no longer trust our cultural guidance in any comprehensive manner. In this situation we must return to our genetic structure and rethink who we are, where we fit into the community of existence, and what our proper role might be within this community."

Thomas Berry, Ph.D. "Ethics and Ecology," paper delivered at Harvard University, 1996

This emerging scientific understanding, and its impact upon us, is slowly coming into the popular mind (for an excellent introduction to the subject, see James Gleick, *Chaos, Making a New Science*, 1987). Not surprisingly, quite a few scientists are beginning to extend the ideas of quantum mechanics and chaos theory to human affairs, to suggest that the place of human beings in the universe is interdependent on the whole system (for example see the work of David Bohm, F. David Peat, Fritjof Capra, Gary Zukav, and Rupert Sheldrake listed in Appendix C). In so doing, these thinkers are finally joining hands with other original thinkers, spiritual leaders on the order of Pierre Teilhard de Chardin, J Krishnamurti, Matthew Fox, and Thomas Berry. Together, these individuals and others like them are projecting a new cosmology.

To grasp the full significance of this large-scale paradigm shift requires considerable diligence and perceptual reorientation on our part. Each of us would be wise to reflect upon its implications. The practice of Reiki supports just such a contemplative enterprise. Before expanding on this, let's take a look at a contextual framework.

Our societal structures and institutions have been based on a model of thinking that sees the world (or would like to see the world) as neatly ordered and composed of parts which act predictably and orderly. This *egocentric* way of looking at the world operates on the assumption that all of the other constituent parts of nature are subject to human control, indeed exist to serve human beings. Human history has been dominated by this assumption—with some disastrous results.

It becomes possible to take an entirely different view on reality by looking at the world from the perspective that existence is full of moments where order disintegrates into chaos, and where chaos in turn births order, where everything cannot be carefully measured and prescribed from without, where humankind instead of ruling the earth and using it for artificial and selfish ends is seen as a part of and not the purpose of nature. Substituting this worldview, this *ecocentric* orientation, for our favored and familiar ones, we can now say we are "*Here*," we are not separate from one another, from the rest of the living natural world, even though surely it appears that we are.

Viewing life in this way puts new emphasis on the importance of understanding the dynamics of the whole system. In a whole system, each part affects and is affected by the whole. This means that in whatever ways you or I, our families, friends, communities, nations, as well as other living creatures act and experience life, all of us are involved, all of us are affected, including Mother Earth herself. And this includes our thoughts, our "consciousness." What we think and believe becomes part of the collective consciousness and dynamically contributes to change and action in the world. Chaos theorists sometimes like to refer to this phenomenon as the "butterfly effect," essentially, the notion that the flapping of the wings of a single butterfly in one area of the world has the rippling effect potential to eventually disrupt or severely alter the weather patterns in another, distant area, even to the point of creating a storm or a tornado. Well, we are all butterflies to one another and to the world we live in. We have a connection and a responsibility to both. To integrate this essential understanding into our everyday lives requires inner vision, inner hearing, and inner heart talk. So, we are talking about a monumental shift in consciousness and understanding.

All significant shifts, because they move us out of the comfortable and the familiar, involve stress, anxiety, even pain. Remember though, pain is the great dissolver of illusion. It can be the impetus for change and balance. Because of pain, we can awaken. We can listen to what is happening and we can let this sink into our consciousness. This in turn allows us to resonate with the ground of all being. Thus we can realize that our challenge is to be open to forces that would keep us in tune with our ultimate purpose and our real concerns.

"Human beings and the Natural World are set on a collision course. If not checked, many of our current practices put at serious risk the future we wish for Human Society, and the Plant and Animal Kingdoms – and may so alter the living world that it will be unable to sustain life in the manner that we know."

The Union of Concerned Scientists "A Warning to Humanity," position paper, 1994

We are in a dialogue with our universe and it is not a one-way conversation. The rest of nature is talking back. Just as I write this, for example, I hear on NPR that global warming has resulted in grass growing in Antarctica (a new phenomenon) and that important weather patterns are being severely interrupted or altered with serious implications for areas in the western hemisphere. Almost daily in the United States we receive dire predictions about the effects of *El Niño* and *La Niña*. These are among the many, many warning messages humankind receives from the universe we inhabit. They are indicators that " something is rotten in the state of Denmark," and, as the old comic strip character, Pogo, might say, "we is it."

Just as obviously, however, there are also numerous indicators that it is us! Some commentators (for example, Robert Sardello, *Facing the World With Soul*) go so far as to suggest that the body's illnesses are metaphors for those of Mother Earth, that the health of individuals is a reflection of the state of health of the rest of the universe. This fits in neatly with the very large group of observers who note that our bodies are in constant communication with us, warn us of toxic imbalances in our systems. This latter understanding is now so well established that it is starting to become a mainstay in the allopathic (traditional) approach to the diagnosis and treatment of illness and disease. Seen in this way, it is not too difficult to conclude that our modern illnesses are a manifestation of our separation from nature and from the natural flow of the universe.

We live in a time when stress, anxiety, and alienation increasingly pervade our being. Our personal whole system— our mind, body, and spirit—is under attack from the pressures and constraints of modern living. It has always been this way to some extent. Life does involve problems. The fight for survival and comfort are constants for all individuals and all societies.

What makes the modern day version of stress and anxiety unique is its intensity. Whatever the benefits of technological advances and changing lifestyle venues, the pressures on contemporary earth dwellers are both incredibly large and relentless. To make matters worse, we have partially lost touch with our most significant ally, our connection to the rest of the natural world. In short, we are alienated from our natural environment and from the natural way of doing things; we are out of joint. I am mindful of the old story about the drunkard who looked for his keys where the light was better, not where they were.

Stay Tuned For Important Messages

Fortunately, our whole system alert mechanisms are paying attention and are constantly sending us messages. These messages, whether communicated physically, emotionally, or mentally, frequently translate into tension somewhere in our bodies. This indicator of mind-body interaction, though alarming, can be positive, for when the interaction goes awry, an opportunity also arises for us to be more attentive to ourselves and to others. We can then re-evaluate and redirect our lives while gaining fresh perspectives. We can focus on our purpose and reconnect with other people and with the rest of the natural environment. All that is needed is a key for unlocking the door to that true potential and one significant, magical key is the practice of Reiki.

The practice of Reiki, an ancient, whole systems, touch therapy practice, was rediscovered and developed by Dr. Mikao Usui, a Japanese physician, in the late 19th and early 20th centuries. Using a simple methodology, Reiki provides the practitioner with the means to calm the turbulent seas of inner and outer being. The practitioner comes to the realization that all humans have a built in capacity to heal and to celebrate life, as well as an extraordinary power to put events in our

"As the nineteenth century closed, belief in reductionist and mechanism prevailed, but the price paid for this was high."

John Briggs and F. David Peat
Turbulent Mirror

lives in context, and thus to understand our symbiotic and participatory role in an unfolding universe.

If we listen to what our bodies communicate to us, we can slip through the barriers of illusion (the predominant *modus operandi*), springboarding through our direct experience of and willingness to learn from stress, to a higher, broader vision of our reality. When one comes to this realization, there is a "rapid reorganization of phenomena," and it relates directly to fully experiencing and celebrating life. But first we have to listen.

What is Your Body Telling You?

"Controlling the state of mind that alters hormone activity has the potential to have an [positive] impact on the immune system."

Dr. Robert E. and Diane Hales
Parade Magazine,
April, 1996

*U*sually, the first place we notice imbalance is in our bodies. It is well documented that stress can prompt abnormal amounts of hormones to flow from the adrenal glands. This shrinks the thymus, which, in turn taxes the whole immune system, setting up a chain reaction. The body becomes susceptible to any number of maladies, but before this happens, your body will give you a wake up call. Or several calls. All you have to do is retrieve your messages and listen. Use the charts on the following pages as a means to decipher your message

Signs of the Times

Recent USA Polls:

❑ **Percentage of people frustrated by the deterioration of the environment: 80**

❑ **Percentage of people dissatisfied with their lives: 74**

❑ **Percentage of people whose doctor visits are stress related: over 70**

❑ **Percentage of high school students suffering from stress: 52**

❑ **Percentage of high school students experiencing suicidal feelings: 25**

Dr. Michael Cohen,
***Reconnecting With Nature*, 1997**

"People who involve themselves in nature reconnecting activities reduce their stress and disorders."

Dr. Michael Cohen,
Reconnecting with Nature

Try This Process:
Body Maps I

When the body signals distress in any or all of the following ways, it can be an opportunity to reevaluate priorities, and to redirect our energies. Check applicable boxes below.

Current Symptom:	Level of Stress You Experience: Light	Moderate	Extreme
Alarm Reactions	☐	☐	☐
Aggression	☐	☐	☐
Anger	☐	☐	☐
Angst	☐	☐	☐
Anxiety	☐	☐	☐
Apathy	☐	☐	☐
Asthma	☐	☐	☐
Back Pain	☐	☐	☐
Blue Moods	☐	☐	☐
Body "Aches"	☐	☐	☐
Boredom	☐	☐	☐
Cancer	☐	☐	☐
Chronic Muscle Strain	☐	☐	☐
Cold Sweats	☐	☐	☐
Confusion	☐	☐	☐
Tension	☐	☐	☐
Depression	☐	☐	☐
Digestion problems	☐	☐	☐
Dizziness	☐	☐	☐
Dry Mouth	☐	☐	☐
Eating Disorders	☐	☐	☐
Excessive Drinking	☐	☐	☐
Fatigue	☐	☐	☐
Grumpy Moods	☐	☐	☐
Headache	☐	☐	☐

"The diamond cannot be polished without friction, nor the man perfected without trials."

Chinese Proverb

	Light	Moderate	Extreme
Heart Arrhythmia	☐	☐	☐
Heart Attack	☐	☐	☐
High Blood Pressure	☐	☐	☐
Hives	☐	☐	☐
Insomnia	☐	☐	☐
Irritability	☐	☐	☐
Loss of Sexual Interest	☐	☐	☐
Melancholy Moods	☐	☐	☐
Overspending, Overeating	☐	☐	☐
Poor Impulse Control	☐	☐	☐
Rashes	☐	☐	☐
Restlessness	☐	☐	☐
Skepticism	☐	☐	☐
Skin Disorders	☐	☐	☐
Sleep Disturbance	☐	☐	☐
Sleeplessness	☐	☐	☐
Temper "Tantrums"	☐	☐	☐
Tightness in Chest	☐	☐	☐
Ulcers	☐	☐	☐
Worrisome Thoughts	☐	☐	☐

Locate your areas of concern on the figures to your right.

Try This Process:
Body Maps II

Now extend the Body Map by noting signs or symptoms of how tension is expressing itself. Indicate these by x= trouble spot or ! = serious concern. Draw a line from each x or ! and make a comment.

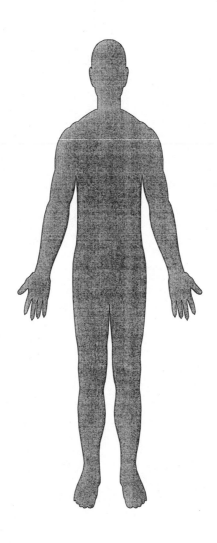

Try This Process:
Body Maps III

Finally, use this page to "map out" in writing areas where mind-body interaction communicates the advisability of change. Take your time, and consider each of the following aspects of your life experience. Then use the spaces below to comment on the current state of affairs in your world.

• **Physical:**

• **Mental:**

• **Emotional:**

• **Relationships:**

• **Inner Spirit:**

Reiki: A Method Which Generates Difference

*W*ithout a method for being mindful of the opportunities that exist within the maelstrom, we may remain closed to really celebrating life. In order to seize the moment while maintaining our equilibrium in the dance of our days, in order to effectively deal with the effects of stress, anxiety, and alienation in our lives, we would be wise to first create a personal sanctuary. Not everyone has a "real, physical" place—a beach house, a remote campsite, a hilltop retreat; but everyone needs and indeed can have a nonphysical destination, a special timeless space upon which to call.

Reiki is just such a place. This tool for relaxation opens new doors of perception to demonstrate both a wonderful ocean of energy and a system for working *with* that energy. The effect is a spacious and exhilarating sense, a state of being. You might describe this as feeling as if you were suspended in a hammock of pure potential.

No retreat for us! No need to hide from the *rigeur*s of modern existence. When life's out of joint, we can consider the possibilities, and Reiki. There are two ways to know Reiki and its possibilities. The first way, experiencing it, is the most important, and many of you may already know Reiki in that manner. You could even become aware of it before you finish this page. However, Reiki is not something that you can "learn" from this book (though you will hopefully learn a lot about it and how to access it). You see, most people who discover Reiki do not start with a book. They start with an *experience*.

The practical meaning of Reiki (as used when it refers to the mindful practice) is a method for touching which generates a difference. The person engaging in the practice knows that something new, and very welcomed, has happened. After you have that experience, even simple things such as reading a book are seen through different eyes. You seem to already know and understand the most important aspects because of that direct experience which addresses and answers the skeptic in all of us.

The second way to know Reiki lies in learning how to evoke the experience; the one that makes you certain that something real, and something refreshing, has happened. You do not have to believe anything in particular to have this learning. You could be like the electrician who does not believe in electrons, but who can wire a building perfectly. Someone who knows how to "plug in" to the practice of Reiki can teach you how.

Just remember: Reiki does not commence with a lot of theory that tells you that if you meditate and exercise for years you will attain a state that you can only imagine now. It starts with the experience. I can assure you: something important happens with Reiki. It happened to me at a time when I was not expecting anything to happen—and it can also happen for you.

Try This Process: A Reiki Place

Journal

Something important happens when you connect with the natural world, something refreshing and healing. Try this exercise to found out what you can learn.

• *Pack a picnic and blankets.*
• *Find a hilltop campsite far from city lights and sounds.*
• *Settle in, watching the earth spin away from the sun ("sunset") and the stars as they appear in the sky.*
• *Lie on your side and look OUT (not up) at the stars.*
• *Now visualize yourself on the curved surface of the Earth—halfway down (not on "top") again looking **out**.*
• *You are part of the planet, held in place by gravity.*
• *Next, arrive at a mental picture of yourself on the bottom of the globe, looking **down** at the stars.*
• *You are an integral part of the cosmos.*
• *What can you learn from this?*

The above is an adaptation from an experiment by Brian Swimme, Ph.D.
The Hidden Heart of the Cosmos.

Try This Process:
Questions For An Interconnected Universe

Read, reflect upon, and note your responses to the following questions.

· *What is the larger significance of the human enterprise in an unfolding universe?*

· *How can we replace traditional ways of seeing the world with those more aligned with the new cosmology?*

· *How can we bridge the vast expanses between the multidimensional realms of body, mind, and inner spirit technology and spirituality?*

· *What is our responsibility to self and others and what is our place in the living global community?*

· *What practical measures are available to restore balance within our microcosmic and macrocosmic realities?*

· *What messages are we putting out to the universe? What is your "butterfly effect?"*

Solutions

"The continuation of life on this planet in a healthy way and within a healthy environment, requires our attitudes encompass all possibilities and that we monitor ourselves responsibly, while continuing to offer ourselves and our gifts to all."

Earlene F. Gleisner, R.N.
Reiki in Everyday Living

In order to solve a problem, we must first understand the problem and then decide on a plan of action. Understanding and determining a program is not a mental activity, not something accomplished by the intellect. Sometimes, if we are willing to just *start where we are*, a path opens up. It may well be that our communal best interest hinges on allotting the timespace to relax into a new understanding of the realities of our existence. These discoveries are just one degree beyond the apparent. They are, however, accessible through the practice of Reiki—and here may begin a journey into energy medicine—for the highest good of all concerned.

Speculate

Question the workings of your universe,
your heart-mind,
and then, question your questions—
for energies design themselves
as different forms of information,
explanations,
not just to scholars trusted, then refined,
but there for all who,
charged with the task of reflecting,
uncovering hidden realms of inner climes,
whilst naked in the glare of individuality,
with singular, unique viewpoints, and thus inclined
to be flexibile, disciplined, permissive in
the full spectrum of bright possibility,
lightly grasp the formulation
of ideas creatively spewed—no, wrenched
from the Core Question.

Wind-in-the-Feather

2

Fortuitous Detours...
Change and Innovation

"listen to this, and hear the mystery inside..."

Rumi

Synchronicity

Today,
not out of planning,
striving
longing
wisdom, or celebrity,
but merely by chance
as I sat in all solemnity
regarding my breath
as it fell and rose,

Today,
a butterfly brushed my nose
and I,
regarding its faerie wings,
beheld, at last,
the Land of Kings!

Wind-in-the-Feather

"The ground of the universe is an empty fullness, a fecund nothingness...the base of the universe seethes with creativity... space- time- foam...."

~ Brian Swimme, Ph.D.
The Hidden Heart of the Cosmos

Signposts and Directions

Sometimes, when one leasts expects it, one's life takes a fantastic turn, as synchronicity plays tricks on stale perceptions, and timing (or luck) present unexpected opportunities for change and innovation. There must have been just such a delightful potential for "being in the right place at the right time" when I encountered a series of fortuitous detours one winter not all that many years ago, and inadvertently awoke to a new vision just one degree beyond the apparent.

I was taking an "inspiration break" (one of the perks self-employment affords me) to motor west with my golden retriever, Maggie. The four-wheeler was packed for adventure, and we headed out in high anticipation of what a long, back-road trip might reveal.

As a management consultant specializing in career and personnel issues, I had plenty on my mind. Business friends I met every day were dropping by the wayside from chronic fatigue, ulcers, burn-out, even heart attacks. I had been gathering statistics for a corporate study, but just recording the facts seemed so futile. I wanted to *do* something about the situation. So while for Maggie this trip meant exotic smells, strange territories, and excellent food in doggie bags, my

"He kept his vigils, likewise,
night after night,
sometimes in utter darkness,
sometimes with a glimmering lamp,
and sometimes, viewing his own face
in a looking glass,
by the most powerful light
he could throw upon it."

Nathaniel Hawthorne
The Scarlet Letter

"The subtle way of the universe
gave birth to a world
of peace and order...
it responds to
the order and harmony
of all beings and things...
without needing to talk ...
without your summoning it,
it comes to you...
without scheming, its plan is perfect
...vast is the subtle energy network
of the universe,
sparsely meshed it is,
yet nothing can slip through it."

Lao Tzu

agenda included: making time for some unscheduled serious thinking; allowing myself to be open to experience; and being willing to follow the signposts as they pointed out new directions.

We set out from Boston in a snow squall, and for the first few days our main objective seemed to be to just keep moving, to find any open road. No sooner would I decide to take one route than heavy snow, sleet, and icy road conditions would change the plan. We followed this zig zag pattern wherever it took us for several days, until gradually we found ourselves headed due south. At the time I can recall having a sense of actually being urged along by some powerful but sure force, and it occured to me that perhaps our fortunes were being controlled by Mother Nature. "Of course, one does not really *expect* to exert control over Mother Nature," I reasoned, between wiper slaps. But it was a novel insight for me that She might be driving, not me. Nonetheless, as Maggie and I continued our southern detour, trying to outrun the freezing cold, only to run into a blizzard that absolutely forbade further travel, I could not escape a sense of destiny. There was nothing to do but to trust the "gods of the changing seasons."

Thus began a charmed voyage—to Santa Fe, New Mexico... and into realm beyond any I had known before.

❖

Santa Fe: Paying Attention

On a steady snowfall, "Good Ole' Gold" and I safely slid into Santa Fe, but we could go no farther. Santa Fe had not been a planned destination—we really didn't have any of these—but here we were. Deciding to capitalize on this unexpected twist of fate, we found lodging, and then set out on foot to absorb the unique ambiance of the town. For some time previously I had been aware of the work of the painter Amado Peña, and read that his work was displayed in a local Santa Fe gallery. I loved Peña's ability to capture the spirit of high desert native peoples. He seemed to be able to soften the boundaries of time, thus allowing us to recognize our kinship in a timeless realm—a very balancing notion. Reflecting on this as we walked towards the gallery, I began thinking how a certain finely crafted silver, coral, and turquoise ring, my "lucky piece," had that quality, too, and smiled to myself as I recalled how it had found its way to me....

Ten years previously, that lucky ring had belonged to Sally, an itinerant crew member of the Western Ice Capades and had been the centerpiece of her "liquid savings account"—handy for trade or barter. It, and other Old Pawn items, rolled snugly in a jewelers bag, had traversed the country. She had acquired the ring in a dramatic way.

As Sally told it, she'd been sitting at the counter in a truck stop near Tucumcari, New Mexico late one night, having a piece of lemon meringue pie, listening to old honky-tonk tunes, and just "minding my own business," when the ring literally had sailed off the gesturing hand of a smooth-shaven cowboy, who was seated next to her. She had already noticed his Stetson hat and his shiny boots, so when the ring dropped with a thud and rolled to a stop within an inch of her cup of coffee, she raised her eyebrows, and smiled openly. Noting her quizzical look, that smooth dude from the prairies "fessed up" as to how he'd won the ring from a pueblo kid in a poker game "back down the road a-piece," and "sorta reckoned" that "maybe it shouldn't even be [his] 'cuz, it once belonged to a medicine man," or at least that's what the kid had told him when he handed it over. "Kinda spooks me," he admitted. Sally immediately thought to herself how nicely it would fit in her little "savings account" jewelers bag. The cowboy "allowed as how the ring sure was too big for him," and told her he did not mind if she "wanted to take it off his hands, since the ring seemed to prefer her, anyway," and he winked at her. Sally returned the favor and the conversation, and pretty soon the ring was hers—"for a fair price." I didn't dare ask what the price was, although her tone of voice suggested that another story lingered there. I found out only that she was pleased that another's folly was her good fortune.

I happened on Sally at a time when she was not working and short on cash. She wanted to trade me something from her Old Pawn collection for money. The moment she unfurled her bag and showed me her treasures, I was struck by the ring. I had the most definite sense that it liked me as much as I liked it! It was almost as if it could sprout little feathery wings and transport itself right into my palm. "That's silly!" I thought, as I negotiated a "fair price." And it wasn't long until I noticed its unique charms, but that is yet another story. Let's just say that I quickly developed an attachment to the ring and came to regard it as my lucky piece. Wherever Janeanne went, there went the ring.

Until that day in Santa Fe, I had never tried to justify my attachment to this remarkable ring, nor to explain the uncanny feeling I had that its story was still unfolding. Now, as Maggie and I threaded our way through the freezing slush on the streets of this historic town, fleetingly, for some inexplicable reason, I found myself wondering if it had once come from a pueblo nearby....

As we sloshed down Palace Avenue towards the oldest public building in the United States, I marveled at how history impresses itself in Santa Fe. Many of the traditional methods which had supplied artifacts of old still flourish, and ancient arts are still practiced by skilled artisans. Some present-day objects are little changed in form and construct from those of a thousand years ago. Looking in the shop windows, I began to connect with the "feel" of these ancient-modern arts, and I found myself wondering if perhaps my ring reflected the same spirit and craftmanship...but wait, here was Peña's place! I halted, transfixed. A canvas, almost the width of a barn door and as tall, greeted me as I entered. Not only was it enormous, but unlike the more subdued pallets of his earlier canvases, this work arrested my attention with its bold strokes and slashes of red. My musings about the ring ceased.

But the Muse would not be denied.

The very next day while icy rains continued to delay travel, the ring once more insisted on inching into my thoughts, when I found myself fascinated with certain small bear carvings of the Zuni tribe. Time and again, my fingers traced the grooves and smooth surfaces of these beautifully executed figures, until I discerned, at last, their appeal to me. That same timeless spirit enveloped these small stone forms too! Most evocative of all were the diminutive pieces of a particular master carver. These came home with me. Something here spoke to my heart as did the whispering ring. Was it just in the execution, I wondered.

The Teacher
"...when the student is ready..."

As chance would have it, a former teacher from Zuni provided the next clue to the ring's evolving tale. She was the owner of a gallery I subsequently visited in Santa Fe. That afternoon found me at her gallery, where we talked at length about her experiences with the Zuni people, their culture and beliefs, including how Zuni fetishes represented archetypal wisdom. After some time, she disclosed that she actually knew the man who had carved the fetishes I had chosen. "He's a blind medicine man whose hands have their own eyes," she reported. "He lives on the Zuni Reservation." As she spoke, my thoughts wandered lightly to that man, and I began trying to visualize in my own mind's eye just how he would carve the intricate bear form. I began wondering how he lived—what his life was like—what it would be like to stay always in one place—how he saw things with an inner sight—and how he could bring such energy into tiny carvings with hands with their own eyes.... Then, suddenly, returning to the moment, and curious to see if the teacher, too, saw the design similarities, I retrieved the bear fetishes from my bag and placed them side-by-side on her ample wooden counter.

"Do you think these are all Zuni pieces?" I inquired. She nodded recognition; they *were* indeed Zuni. Next I produced the ring, intending to ask if she thought it were Zuni too, but before I could, I heard her draw in a sharp breath. She seemed so startled that I proceeded to tell her what I knew of the ring's story. "There's much more to it," she ventured, and then urged me to travel to the Zuni Reservation. Something in me said, "Onward!" and when I agreed to go, she headed into her office humming mysteriously. She reappeared a short time later bearing two sealed envelopes in hand, and asked that I deliver them. One was to a friend of hers—the other was for the blind artist. Then, with a glowing smile and a hug, she sent me on my way, her eyes twinkling with untold delight.

I had made myself a promise to be "open to opportunity" and "willing to follow signposts" along the way. Mother Nature had made the travel arrangements and now Zuni called. As I turned out the light in my hotel room that evening, the words of the Teacher played over and over in my mind: "There's more to it… There's more to it…" and soon a medicine man of inner sight smiled to himself and sang in my dreams… as a spider spun a golden web.

Early the next day, bearing messages to her friend, and to the one who had carved my bear fetishes, Golden-One-With-Wagging-Tail and I set out for Zuni. It was the first sunny day that week. The roads were clear.

In the gentle morning hours, the lands surrounding Santa Fe always appear full of melody and movement. Undulating hills breathe shadows. The landscape resounds with a beat of its own, and the wind murmurs tones known only in the high desert. Aromas of piñon pine and sage, with which the air is ever pungent, complement a scene of uncluttered vegetation. This is all perfectly punctuated with an infinite variety of striking landforms. These, not duplicated in any other part of the world, greet the ascending sun, jutting their points into azure skies, as if they wish to release the deepest hues of blue to spread across the country with dazzling intensity. On this morning, however, through all this beauty and all this energy, there emerged in me a sense of cosmic belonging and profound gratitude. I was on a special journey, and while I wasn't sure about who was driving, I knew I was along for the ride!

Maggie, with ears and nose twitching, perched expectantly on the passenger seat of the trusty four-wheeler. She was excited. We were both excited. "Hands have their own eyes," I told her, and speculated about what lay before us in Zuni.

Zuni: Emptying

*W*e wound our way past the Rio Grande, toward the southwest sector of New Mexico and the Zuni Reservation. Hours later, the road opened to a small town of weathered, one-story buildings lining the main street. Even though I felt as though I, as an individual, had been encouraged to come here, I also wondered whether we were but intruders in these lands, which have been home for the Anasazi Nation and its children for thousands of years.

Spotting the address the Teacher had given me, I found a parking space and emerged from my vehicle, messages and heart in hand. Maggie padded along beside me, attentively. She planted herself, resolutely, by the doorway of the artists' co-op that was my destination. Breathing deeply, I crossed the threshold. Maggie's eyes followed me.

All activity within the work room ceased, as I entered, alone. Ten pairs of Zuni eyes regarded me closely, and within that suspenseful instant I had a fleeting vision of another time when the Spaniard, Coronado, had led an expeditionary force in gilded armor (with metal helmets sporting plumes) against the unarmed, peace-loving, Zuni farming communities. It saddened me to think how exploitation from outsiders has characterized Zuni history, and how more recent times have witnessed invaders of another kind. These modern invaders who plunder sacred ruins, and who, armed with videocams and bent on aggressive sight-seeing, treat the Zuni like zoo animals available for their viewing pleasure. There was tension in the air.

"I was hoping to speak with the master carver," I began, tentatively. "I have messages from the Teacher in Santa Fe." A senior member of the group approached me. I handed her the first note for the Teacher's friend. She read it, folded it, and put it in the pocket of her business suit, without uttering a word. Then excusing herself politely, she returned to the others (all women in skirts or jeans). There ensued animated conversation, gasps, and glances in my direction as she relayed information, and I felt increasingly self-conscious. I could feel my pale skin turning various shades of crimson as those dark eyes looked at me once more. Then in a fluid movement, she turned and spoke with authority. "He is not here. But, you are welcome. Please come in," she said pleasantly. "Apparently, our friend in Santa Fe views you as a sister of the Bear Clan."

I smiled in relief and nodded, hoping she didn't notice my changing skin tone, unsure as to what she meant by "sister of the Bear Clan," but appreciative of the acceptance. Though trembling, I managed to hand over the other note written to the carver. She then guided me across the roughly finished floor to what looked like a one-time grocery display case containing a sizable array of his creations.

Now she seemed to have taken on the same glow as the Teacher in Santa Fe, as she deftly removed an elegant rock-red fetish from the top shelf. Even from a distance, I could see that every detail was hand-perfected, each curve blending blending flawlessly into the next. Even the turn of the carved head was alert. How I longed to know how hands could have eyes of their own. "The Old Carver would want you to have this bloodstone bear," the woman suddenly announced. "He finished it last night and brought it with him when he came in with his family earlier today." As I started to decline, she placed her hand on mine and continued….

"You know, many years ago a "certain ring"—finely-crafted, silver, coral and turquoise, and handed down from a medicine elder—was gambled away in a poker game to a cowboy in a Stetson hat. Is it true that you know this story?"

"Good Heavens!!" I exclaimed, stunned by the question.

A dizzying realization was sweeping over me, as my recently red skin turned to a bloodless white. My heart and mind struggled to assimilate the meaning of that moments—of coincidence and fate—of trust and letting go—of finding needles in haystacks—and of lucky charms which sprouted feathery wings.

I had carried that knowledgeable ring with me every day for years. It had accompanied me as I won consulting contracts with IBM, Hewlett Packard, and Sun Microsystems; indeed, whenever I made senior-level presentations. It always jangled in my bag, reminding me of a universe of abundant blessings —an ungainly lucky token in one sense, but clearly more than just a charm. It had come to be a symbol of personal integrity to me. As such, it served as a reminder of my connection the spiritual universe.

If this ring had a "special energy," it now also had a fairy tale story, for after all these years (and a few detours) *it had found its way back to the place where it belonged!*

I stood speechless. From a place deep within me, I knew that the time had come for me to release it. But could I do it? Could I detach from my fondness for it, from my possessing it, and the feeling of security it represented, to celebrate its enchanting "homing" powers?

As the Zuni woman's warm hand placed the now warm bloodstone fetish in mine, I knew what I must do. I tugged the equally warm prodigal ring from my bag, and deposited it carefully in her open palm. As if from a distant earthwalk I heard myself say, "If this ring can find its way home, so can we all."

Looking back on that moment, I realize that a chord was struck within me; a coming together, a gentle untethering in the sound of a heartbeat.

I was coming to see the potential that opens for us as we release absolutes. I was coming to understand that trusting the process, in concert with paying attention, leads to a new level of perception and awakening. Then things seem to sort themselves out, find their places and balance.

And, oh what a joy it is to discover that when you relinquish that which you prize, things of even greater significance appear.

Potentiality

In the marvelous, swirling, dancehall of life, one thing inevitably leads to another in a chain reaction of coincidence and consequence and new cohesion. Late that day, leaving the town of Zuni, I was especially mindful of the phenomenon of unfolding. I was especially mindful of possibilities.

As my furry friend and I bumped along across Route 264 towards Window Rock, Ganado, and the mesas of the Hopi lands on our way to Sedona, Arizona, I simply absorbed the incredible wonders of this land of enchantment. Somehow, somewhere in the recesses of my being, I was aware of an emergence, even a metamorphosis. Indeed, the very scene before us augured change. Giant saguaro cacti arose from scrub, to paint living hieroglyphs against a sky shading from azure to magenta. For hours, the shifting colors emblazoned their presence upon my consciousness, as the artist within me celebrated the unbounded energy of the place, and presented me with a shift in vision.

Eventually and gradually the western horizon called the sun home. It was very quiet now, and chilly. A hawk circled above, and I felt a majestic emptiness within my being. Now, a family of cottonwood trees beckoned us to the side of the road, where, snuggled up in a traveling blanket next to that nice warm dog who seemed to know my every notion, I enjoyed profound inner stillness. Here, in these ancient lands, I sank into sleep like a child at its mother's heart, and when I awoke hours later to gaze on a full moon, and to hear the distant baying of a wolf, it was as if I were awakening for the first time. Somehow the exchange at Zuni had released me to know in new ways.

I began to recognize the *experience* of an all-at-once, nonlinear, almost fluid awareness. This magic day, highlighted by my visit to the bear clan and by my relinquishing of the ring to its proper place—a "special place" of simply being, and not judging or questioning—assured me that all manner of things become suddenly possible. I can remember thinking, "If only there were a way to share this feeling with every person in the world."

Sedona: Pure Potential

*D*awn. Filtered sunlight. Crisp air. Frozen dew drops. The canyons buzzed with life. Sedona, Arizona carved her way into one of these, just around the curve. Maggie and I had departed our night's lodgings in Flagstaff, to navigate the serpentine route through the Oak Creek Canyon and Verde Valley, just thirty miles away, in time for breakfast. A small café soon crept into view. Adjacent to the café, an interesting rock shop caught my eye. "Hmmm!" It looked perfect for a minor league rockhound (like me) whose "Grampaw" had taught her about fossils and mineral formations, and in the process had passed on his taste for treasure hunting.

Grampaw and I had relished finding many colorful glinty, geometrically-shaped crystals, and we had always anticipated the uncovering of "the one" we had never found. So, on this day, with inherited zeal, the goal was to perpetuate the legacy of "The Search," the quest for a true rarity. I was ready. After Zuni, I expected the unexpected. I *expected* bounty!

Still riding serendipity's wave, and forgetting all about breakfast, while Maggie settled down on the back seat, I entered the rock shop. A pretty woman of perhaps thirty emerged, all aglow, from behind boxes of huge chunks of rough stones, and smaller pieces of polished stones. Her smile was friendly. Something in it reminded me of those I'd found in Zuni. Maybe it was the openness. We connected right away, talking about rocks and minerals, treasure hunting, travels, and good fortune. This was Joan Marie, who confided that she also was a rockhound. Whenever she got the chance (which wasn't too often these days since her own business was flourishing), she helped out at the store. That way, she explained, she got to meet the miners who supplied it and to have a first look at their "finds." She knew much more than I did about mining, that was for sure, but I soon discovered that she also knew a lot more about crystal formations. She saw these as representative of a universe of order.

She had recently come to understand this quite clearly, she confided, when she realized that crystals, indeed all things in the Cosmos, are sustained and organized through forces of attraction. I had already observed how crystals can grow in water. What she said made sense.

"How did you figure this out?" I asked, and was told that she'd had a "shift in awareness" that seemed to flow from the process of opening up to an extended sense of perception in a nonverbal, nonlinear experience she had discovered called Reiki. This left her mind (and to some extent, mine as I listened) exploding with the possibilities of a world, interconnected, and evolving itself through loving attraction.

"Reggae," I repeated, thinking how odd it was to have come to such numinous conclusions while dancing.

"No, no, not Reggae," she laughed uproariously, as if tickled to her bones, "Reiki, Ray-KEE." Without giving me a chance to get a question in edgewise she continued.

"You see," she said brightly, "knowing that we are absolutely, always, at every moment, connected in a natural process inspires me! I like the idea of swimming in a sea of energy, knowing I "am" it; knowing that I have never been apart from it, even when I have thought I was; knowing that the separateness exists only in my mind, and nowhere else; knowing that the separateness is an illusion...."

"Well, I'm not so sure about that!" I responded.

Her reply was swift and sure.

"This is based on fact, not on my philosophy or on hoping or dreaming! Science, quantum physics, general systems theory, astronomical theory, and mysticism all confirm that we are part of one vast universal chain of being — from the tiniest rose quartz crystal to the most distant star in the spiraling galaxies…" and her voice trailed off, caught up in her own wonderment. I took advantage of this lull in the conversation to slip in my question.

"What's Reiki?" I asked meekly.

Now that Joan Marie was just as clever as a certain Zuni ring. She wound her way around the subject until I was fairly bursting with curiosity.

"Ya' know," she mused, "I think that our problem is that we've just plain forgotten the Law of Concentrated Focus, and so we've also forgotten how to tap into Pure Potential!"

"What on God's Green Earth are you talking about?" I asked, puzzled.

"Oh!" she grinned, looking directly into my eyes, "would you like me to explain Reiki to you?"

*A*fter the drama of the previous day, I was primed, very open to appreciating whatever the universe had to offer. And curious, always curious. With another round of questions and answers, I discovered that Joan Marie and her husband were licensed physical therapists who had a practice there in Sedona. They specialized in "stress reduction therapy for wellness." Rather than attempt to explain Reiki to me, Joan Marie insisted that all that was necessary, was for me to *"experience"* Reiki. To *experience* Reiki, she explained, required only that I bring myself to their studio that afternoon where I would discover something akin to a gentle touch massage, which would be deeply relaxing.

Was it just a coincidence that I happened upon Joan Marie on this trip of fortuitous detours? What do you think? She had offered me this opportunity to *experience,* first hand, a new way to relax—just what I was looking for—Reiki: it sounded promising. Opportunity in the form of a treat!

"I accept!"

Reiki and Relaxing: Creative Potential

Joan Marie's studio was a tribute to rock lovers, plant lovers, and lovers of sound and scent. She had created an environment using nature's tools which was soft, comfortable, and warm. Reclining on a cushioned table, and putting aside my "agenda," I began to notice a welcomed easing of tension in this hospitable space. Joan Marie had just completed her "First Degree Reiki Training," and seemed very pleased to have found a candidate so open to and interested in her discovery. Little did she know the level of anticipation I had already reached. Nevertheless, here I was exploring foreign territory—far, far from the "normal" confines of the corporate comfort zone. This was mysterious stuff, and definitely one degree beyond my norm.

Intrigued I was, but with this, my very first *experience* with Reiki, my strong interest and curiosity changed to astonishment. As I closed my eyes and Joan Marie commenced the session, I began to *see* (with inner sight I didn't know I possessed) the vivid colors of yesterday's drive across New Mexico, only they were intensified. The emotional magnitude of the whole day's experience touched my heart once more, and I was acutely mindful of the present moment, the timeless moment, of then, and now, and again. This "extended sense of perception" was entirely new to me. "What did it mean," I asked myself?

Joan Marie had first placed her hands just above my eyes, then, after a few minutes, moved her hands to the right and left of my temples. As her hand positions changed, time seemed to melt away. *I relaxed, deeply.* With the deeper, slower breathing, a rhythmic thought pulsed through me: "our essence is energy," it said. When the hour (a whole hour?!...) had slipped away, any remaining doubt had departed. I felt terrific! This I expressed gratefully.

Joan Marie smiled and said, "My Native American friends refer to the feeling of connectedness in Reiki as 'Itaki,' 'Spider Medicine,' the golden web that connects all things. Reiki gives us a wonderful opportunity to see how this can be so."

"If you feel drawn to the experience," she suggested, "go ahead and look up a Reiki practitioner/teacher and learn to practice Reiki yourself. You might find *your hands have eyes of their own.*"

A Path to Relaxation

We live by the water in the Great Pacific Northwest. An island in Puget Sound is our home, and it is to this shore we return, time after time.

After a long assignment back East and three weeks on the road with its many fortuitous detours, it was gratifying to sight the "homeplace." The Pacific Northwest is famous for mystical, lingering mists and its grey winter skies. Yet on this particular moonlit December ride, as the ferry glided silently between islands, the holiday lights of Friday Harbor reflected a bright mood in the black waters, which I could feel to the depths of my being. We had arrived home safely—with gifts for our Island friends. Peña prints. Southwest artifacts. Bear fetishes. A few doorstoppers, even, in the form of polished rocks. There were also many wonderful stories to tell, and there was even a special present from Joan Marie—a gift certificate for another Reiki session!

Within the week, I touched base with a local Reiki Master of *The Usui System of Reiki*. Willingly venturing this time one degree beyond my norm, I stood poised on the threshold of discovery with enthusiastic expectations. I was aware of the reemergence of the glow I had come to know so well in Sedona, as I told my new Teacher of the many "happy accidents" that had led me to her doorstep. I asked her many questions, and was impressed with her wholeheartedness. Here was a seasoned professional, an R.N. with a Masters Degree in Medical Social Work, who had been teaching Reiki for years. She explained that her own teacher was Phyllis Furumoto, who was initiated by Takata, who had been taught by Hayashi, the appointed successor to Usui, the Founder! I gathered that this was her lineage, her bona fides. Obviously, she was proud to share them with me.

"Reiki is a gift you give yourself," I can still hear her telling me. "The practice assists you in cultivating your own ability to attune to your own physicality and energetics through initial, and then more specialized trainings called 'First' and 'Second' Degrees. If you invest yourself in the practice, you will find that it not only relieves stress, and promotes well-being, but can give you a whole new perspective on the meaning of life!"

"I guessed that," I replied, confidently.

She invited me to attend a weekend seminar, during which I would receive training in the initial practice, and qualify for my Reiki I certification.

That sounded fine to me, but "what about Second Degree?" I asked. She laughed gently, and said, "Oh, my goodness, don't be in such a rush! It takes time to assimilate this training! You are moving into *energy medicine* here, and there are learning curves and adjustment periods just as in any other discipline or artform. As a matter of fact," she continued, "our professional association officially recommends that you wait a minimum of several months [before moving on to the Second Degree level]."

Obviously, there was more to Reiki than I had suspected. So, for now, I would try "Reiki I Training." I would consider her advice and wait to see if I wanted to go further.

My business pals in Boston, Detroit, Chicago, San Francisco and Seattle, firmly inured in the competitive (subject/object) business view, had assured me that "relaxation" was of topic of great interest to them, but had forgone "doing something about relaxing" for themselves. When I told them of my upcoming training and of my initial *experience*, they wondered if it wasn't all just "too good to be true." But my intuition, as well as that brief, direct *experience* with Reiki, told me that my optimism was warranted and that the upcoming Reiki seminar held exciting prospects—for us all.

The very next weekend found me ferrying to neighboring Orcas Island for the weekend seminar. Rain poured down in massive, strident, clattering sheets, but inside the log cabin where Takata herself had once stayed, a fire was burning in the stone fireplace and it was warm and dry. A medical doctor, an author, several nurses and two computer "nerds" would be taking Reiki I Training with me, as we all began treading a new path to relaxation. And so, even though it still seemed a bit strange and mysterious to one who generally wore business attire and carried a brief case, I trusted the "happy accidents" that had brought me here. *"What magic can manifest itself," I wondered, "when one dares to explore beyond the usual and the apparent?"*

Belonging

In recent years, the field of industrial psychology has paid particular attention to statistics regarding the correlation between employee effectiveness and stress management. Research indicates that those who choose to ignore the physical and nonphysical signs of pressure get sick more frequently than do those who know how to alleviate stress. This is a familiar enough concept, as noted in Chapter One. However, upon completion of initial training in the Reiki methodology, the stress/disease connection often becomes clear in *a new way*. One comes to understand that this is not about remote statistical analyses—this is about taking personal responsibility for wellness, beginning with the self, and extending to all the other natural elements of our universe. It is about being open to viewing one's relationship to one's environment in holistic ways, about accepting the notion of *global wellness* as something directly related to you.

You do not have to be a rocket scientist to appreciate the statistics which say that it is smart to engage in some regular relaxation practice. And, once you have *experienced* it, you do not have to go through any mental gymnastics to figure out that the Reiki *experience* puts you in contact with a different perspective. Rather, you "know it" because you have *experienced* it. It then becomes just good common sense to include the practice of Reiki in your everyday life style. The practice of Reiki offers limitless possibilities and an invigorating perspective. Luckily, amidst the myriads of available stress management techniques and alternative approaches, I had stumbled upon one with which I felt at home and which I have practiced every day since that first class. With this practice has come a new sense of inner and outer balance—truly a new outlook on life. For me, Reiki I Training proved to be a window of opportunity for relaxation, for creative inspiration, and for a clear sense of connectedness to the rest of living

"When we are unhurried and wise
we perceive
that only great and worthy things
have any permanent
and absolute existence -
that petty fears,
and petty pleasures
are but the shadow of reality."

Henry David Thoreau

creation. One comes finally to understand about "belonging."

I have found that when you create a comfortable space for yourself and you allow yourself to expect a quieting, you engage a *process*. You thereby set in motion a dynamic energy that releases tension, and can bring about, and sustain, a sense of improved mind-body-inner-spirit integration. As a result, you are activating your own natural healing mechanism! You feel good—at home with yourself in the universe.

Think of it. Reiki training and practice helps you to connect with the best things about yourself—constantly reminds you of your "resplendent personage." To the extent that you allow it to happen, you can open to your potential as both a physical and energetic creature. The more you come to a new appreciation of your competence and vitality, the more quickly tautness, on many levels, slackens. This works synergistically to create positive momentum towards undoing tension all around you. Your dedication to the practice of Reiki has big rewards. But first, set foot on the path.

The discussion of my personal journey is set out here as but one example among many. For me, it was magical, at times almost surreal. It is still so today, each day filled with acceptance, openness—and discovery. All journeys have this same potential. They needn't be so dramatic as my experiences in New Mexico and Arizona. For some of you, they may be even more dramatic. Certainly, your story will have its own remarkable touches and special experiences and signposts, its own excitement and dynamics.

Earth, Air,
Fire and Water
Seek justice
through
Simplicity and Reverence.
They need Us so!

Wind-in-the-Feather

Try This Process: A
Your Experience Counts!

What fortuitous detours led you to explore beyond the apparent?

- **When did they occur?**

- **Where were you at the time?**

- **Why were you looking beyond the obvious?**

- **How did you discover new ways of seeing?**

Try This Process: B
Expectations

As you explore beyond the apparent, what do you expect to find in the following areas?

Physical:

Mental:

Emotional:

Relationship:

Inner Spirit:

Energetic:

3

About Reiki

"I remind myself that my inner and outer life depends on
the labors of other men, living and dead, and that I must
exert myself in order to give in the measure as I have
received and am still receiving."

Albert Einstein

Interweaving

If you
put aside
the ladder of your
discontent to
step forth, trusting
upon the path
that is a spiral,
leading to the other
paths which
curl their way with
yours,
in and out -
until your journey
expands,
through
interweaving,
will you not reach
"Beyond?"

Wind-in-the-Feather

"...a great change is stirring..."

~ Hawayo Takata*

Room for Change

𝒜 motley crew of individuals from assorted backgrounds and corporate career paths assembled. We were ready to make a personal investment in some form of relaxation. The meeting place was a small conference room on the third floor of the office building where we all worked. It was equipped with an oblong table, a dozen chairs, and an overhead projector. This grey-toned inside room buzzed with the sound of fluorescent lights, and possessed the aura of a dank cell. There were no windows, no sun, or fresh breezes, or bird songs to distract or remind us of our connection with the rest of life. A plastic water jug sat on its tray in the center of the table, surrounded by white polystyrene cups—offerings on the altar of consumer manipulation.

We were a small group held together by a common desire to develop an alternative approach for releasing *tension* in our workplace. We were all aware that there were numerous other methods of dealing with stress "out there" (meditation, exercise, "downers," martinis, escapism, counseling). Indeed, many of us had experimented with one or more. What we were looking for, however, was something simple, something not too expensive or time-consuming, something we could use conveniently on site. It had now been almost exactly a year since I had undergone my initial Reiki Training, and was eager to share with the group a practice that I *knew from*

"The greatness of the role a man has played in this world cannot always be estimated by the size of his tomb or the height of his monument."

Henry Haynie
Paris, Past & Present

*See Appendix A

experience could work. I had prepared an informal talk and was excited, though a little nervous, about the prospect of being an agent for change for my co-workers.

At the start of the meeting, I excused myself briefly and left the room, only to appear again a few minutes later accompanied by an odd-sized piece of furniture—a massage chair, of about standard in height, but with dips, curves, and special holes in it—and a surprise guest, a Reiki therapist who would demonstrate Reiki. "Show and Tell time!" I announced and smiled. Supported by the presence of an experienced teacher, I was now quite ready to share what facts I knew about the practice, and especially about *the experience* of Reiki. A "hands-on" demonstration was about to begin.

That meeting was the first of many on my road to becoming a Reiki teacher. Now, more than ten years later, and a Reiki Master myself, I am honored to share this information with you! This is the subject of the chapter that follows. In this chapter we take a look at some of the most frequently asked questions about *The Usui System of Reiki*.

Questions

Who teaches the Reiki methodology?
Where will I find the right teacher for me?
What should I expect from such a teacher?
What is the point of regular Reiki practice?
What is the conceptual basis of Touch for soothing within Reiki?
Who can practice Reiki?
What does Reiki training cost?
How does the Reiki methodology compare to other techniques?

Reiki Touching

*W*hat is your first instinct when you twist the wrong way and feel a twinge of pain? "Yikes!" you sputter, and put your hands on the offended spot. And when a little child is feverish, do you not instinctively place your hand gently upon the child's forehead? When loving folks meet, this is one thing they commonly do: they touch, hug, hold hands. You have probably noticed how even dogs and cats and all sorts of furry and feathered creatures poke, prod, nuzzle, and touch in greeting. *Touching is just natural.*

In his book *Touching, The Human Significance of the Skin*, Ashley Montagu, prolific writer on all facets of human development, says that the communications we transmit through touch "constitute the most powerful means of establishing human relationships, [and are] the foundation of experience." In the same vein, Montagu notes that during periods of stress, "the need for body contact...may become intensified...." These facts are well documented, both by extensive research and, for most of us, by our everyday experiences. Is it any wonder then that a large number of individuals and even groups of people have dedicated their lives towards developing and teaching the art of touch for healing purposes? The rediscovery and development of Reiki over the period of the last one hundred years or so is a reflection of exactly that impulse. Reiki is indeed a touching healing therapy practice—but with a twist.

Reiki differs from other nontraditional approaches to healing touch in two signicant ways, both involving a different sense of the word "touch." The first concerns the range of healing possibilities. For the Reiki practioner, touching is a *natural* and simple response to any number of circumstances, not simply to situations involving physical illness and injury. Second, and perhaps more startling to someone learning about Reiki for the first time, the "heal-ing" associated with the

"To me, Reiki is prayer in action. The Reiki practitioner is a flute for the Divine to play through; that energy of balancing which sings healing."

Songbird,
Longtime Reiki Master

practice of Reiki does not necessarily have to involve physical touching (though it may and frequently will). What is necessary, and therefore common to all Reiki *experiences*, however, is *and exchange of, or a shift in, energy*. Moreover, the circumstances related to the use of Reiki do not necessarily require either the physical presence or the active participation of the recipient.

Simply put, the Reiki methodology is a straightforward and uncomplicated technique for balancing energy to assist in the healing process across all areas of need. Anyone experiencing this energy exchange or shift becomes initiated in a new understanding of the healing powers extant in all humankind and their own potential to be an instrument of change for themselves and others. Once learned, Reiki is an effective tool that you can carry with you and use all of your life. It can bring you a heightened awareness of the integration tendancy (the action of healing) we all possess. You may even experience a whole-hearted sense of your deep connections with the Universe.

In the act of learning Reiki you become both the guest and the provider of a banquet of life-affirming delights. You empower yourself as a living being, interconnected with other living beings in a vibrant energy field, to nurture yourself and others.

"That which is not, shall never be; that which is, shall never cease to be, to the wise, these truths are self-evident."

Bhagavad Gita,
400 B.C.

About Finding a Teacher

*Y*ou may have become interested in the practice of Reiki because you *experienced* it. You may suspect or realize that it is an effective tool for tension relief and for processing stress. Soon, however, you may come to find that Reiki offers more than this.

As Sharon L. Van Sell, R.N., Ed.D., describes in the February, 1996 issue of *RN Magazine*, Reiki generates strong testimonials from patients with AIDS, lupus erythematosus, chronic pain, and a host of other conditions. She writes that double blind, randomized clinical trials and lab reports confirm the positive results. Says Van Sell, "Whether you (nurses) work in an acute care facility, or attend patients who need long-term care, Reiki therapy gives you the tools needed to minister to physical, emotional and spiritual needs."

If you have had a memorable Reiki *experience*, or through ongoing therapeutic sessions have come to enjoy Reiki's potential for alleviating stress, and you have not already taken Reiki training, you may want to learn this methodology for its energizing, integrating, or healing effects. The time may even come when you will want to explore deeply into the practice. In any case, please consider this wise advice: One of the first requirements, if one is interested in commencing or continuing the study of *any* artform, is that "one finds one's own teacher." So it is with *The Usui System of Reiki.*

Remember your favorite teachers throughout the years— those you liked, and respected, and who took a personal interest in you? In your pursuit of Reiki, look for nothing less than this. Do not compromise! Do not settle for second best! Honor yourself by looking for one who is genuine, for that person may become a gateway for you. Ask difficult questions of this person. *(When can you speak to yourself from the center of the Universe?)* Ask about your prospective teacher's philosophy, Reiki experiences, and how long it took this person to become a Master. * What aspects

"Tranquility! thou better name
Than all the family of Fame."

Samuel Taylor Coleridge

of mastery does this person demonstrate? Remember, you are looking for a teacher with a foundation of comprehensive training and practice in the rich tradition of Reiki, one who is a able to blend aspects of the training with discussion and interaction in an environment that encourages you to integrate what you learn into everyday life.

Since there are many Reiki Masters all over the globe (including some not of *The Usui System of Reiki*), finding *a* teacher is not a problem. What might be challenging is connecting with *the* one for you.** In this sense, your search may be quite arduous. It could discourage those who lack stamina or enthusiasm. Over the years I have come to see that only those who are really drawn to an artform delve into it—and Reiki is no different. Really wanting the understanding is probably what ensures success in connecting with a guide and mentor.

> "But always, it seems we have a duty to come to greater discernment about our path, about its meaning, about how we walk it."
>
> Beatrix Murrell,
> Essayist

Once you have found *the* teacher, learning the Reiki methodology will not be difficult. Once you have learned it, you will be pleased to find how easily this relaxation practice blends into your daily routine. You can tailor it to fit your individual needs. You can share it. You can present yourself with a simple, readily accessible focal point for dissolving stress and for attaining new perspectives, always no farther removed than your fingertips. This may unfold into an avenue for exploring and developing your innate resources. Interestingly, as they say: "When the student is ready, the teacher will appear."

In the meantime, keep your eyes and ears open, do some research and follow your inner guidance. Many people have participated in Reiki relaxation over a period of time before taking the Training themselves. Some folks prefer to continue with Reiki as participants (as opposed to practitioners) and that's just fine. In either case, you can experience *energy medicine*, and thus touch-in to a new sense of your real connectedness with an energetic system. In this experience, an alternative way of perceiving and negotiating in both the physical and energetic worlds opens to you.

---

*   *See Appendix A for interviewing questions for a prospective Reiki teacher.*

**   *To find a Reiki master of the Usui lineage, try Appendix A.*

About Costs

$\mathcal{A}$ program of Reiki therapy in which bi-weekly or weekly sessions focus on relaxation may be on your agenda. If so, the costs will be in the range of $30 to $50 per hour. Most therapists work on a sliding scale and are open to making arrangements. In Reiki Training Seminars, learners prepare themselves for deeper involvement in not only Reiki practices and potentials, but also what it means to be truly connected with the flow and energy of the universe. These also involve fees, but costs are reasonable.

Fees represent an energy exchange; demonstrate a level of commitment to the living community; and honor the dedication of Reiki Masters to the work and teaching of Reiki, as expressed in their years of study and training in a mentored relationship with a Master.

There is in the Buddhist tradition a ritual of honoring harvest. The peasant would bring a bowl of his finest rice to place at the feet of the ancestor who oversaw the harvest. This gift was not the dregs, but the most excellent portion which the peasant offered back to his heritage, to the earth, and to all that is. Similarly, *The Usui System* views the energy exchange as an honoring process. "Honoring" could include any number of your valued services or bartered goods, or money viewed as "concretized energy."

In this exchange, we are affirming a practice of *being* in abundance, self-empowerment, and of commitment to engaging Life by focusing upon the *potential to manifest a creative view that encompasses one's natural inclination towards abundance.*

$\mathcal{F}$ocusing attention upon and activating the potential for stress relief is not the only benefit of Reiki Training. It can also help to provide the practitioner with a new way of looking at the world as a whole system—in a holistic worldview.

"Takata stressed...
that you can do things
from the kindness of your heart,
but it is also good for the other person
to have an opportunity
to give in return.
It did not need to be much—
a loaf of bread, a jar of jam,
a bag of fruit from their own trees,
a work exchange or money.
It would be an appreciation
of the times spent [which]...
might otherwise have been spent
working for the family,
and then no one
would be shortchanged."

Wanja Twan,
In the Light of a Distant Star

Try This Process:
Your Personal Growth Timespace Budget

Examine items below. Fill in information and draw conclusions.

Hour:	Personal Growth Timespace	Personal Growth $$
Physical needs/desires:		
Mental needs/desires:		
Emotional needs/desires:		
Relationship needs/ desires:		
Inner spirit needs/desires:		
Community activities:		
Global concerns:		

Conclusions:

Self-management directive:

Try This Process:
Where do YOU Fit In your Monthly $$ Budget?

Tally the expenses in "A" below, then compare those to $$ allotted for "B," Personal Growth.

Item:	Expense:
A **Mortgage/Rent:**	
Food:	
Utilities:	
Transportation:	
Supplies:	
Fixed Expenses:	
Entertainment:	
	Total:
B **Personal Growth Timespace:**	**Total:**

Reiki Training Seminars

In the **Reiki I Training Seminar** (usually taught in four three-hour sessions), for example, students *experience* their relationship to the whole by starting with the study of the physical body and its systems in a tangible, three-dimensional sphere. Class participants familiarize themselves with Reiki movements, consisting of methodical hand placements. Here students learn about the correlation of various "message centers" of the body. Finally, in a participatory segment of the training, a sense of the artform and potential of Reiki may emerge.

First Degree Reiki Training also introduces the student to the inspirational story of the originator of the Reiki methodology, Dr. Mikao Usui. This story serves as a model for integrating Reiki, and whole systems thinking into one's life. In subsequent training sessions, students become familiar with how the practice of Reiki may induce relaxation on many levels. The basic seminar, however, lays the foundation of format and form and provides, through an effective mentoring process, a personal support system for the learner.

The **Reiki II Training Class** is designed for those who wish to explore deeply a practical technique for cultivation tenderness and compassion for self and others. Here, students learn how to work with multidimensional aspects of being, and with subtle energy. Mentoring, begun in Reiki I training, continues.

The Reiki II Class (which usually takes place in two sessions) is meant for those who are dedicated to integrating Reiki into their lives in a much fuller fashion. These practitioners, having come to see the interconnected nature of all living beings, resolve now to share with their community, both local and global, the ongoing practice of the artform. They develop many of the skills necessary to participate more fully in global nurturance through contemplative focus. Students also learn how to work with mental and emotional aspects of being, and a system by which energy is transferred.

A Ripening Process

When an artform or tradition begins with emphasis exclusively on technical skills and practices and centers its energies around *procedure*, it can get distorted, even trivialized. In such situations, it becomes possible for the artform and much of its significant message to get lost. Hence, a methodology of power is apt to emerge; a methodology that is subject to forgetting or denying the simple *experiencing* of the artform. This type of approach to transformation (which is not simple), glorifies rules or the "correct way of doing things," and thus frequently underplays the very important ripening process that is the fruit borne from awareness, reflection, and commitment. The potentials for this happening are particularly present in unmentored training, or in any training that mistakenly focuses upon the "doing and the ways of doing," as opposed to "being and the ways of being," and it is a potential danger with all transformational philosophies and practices— even Reiki. So prospective Reiki learners need to be aware of these possibilities and choose their learning and their teachers carefully. Learn to ask questions. Listen to the answers and get a real feel for the answerer.

Just as when learning to prepare a gourmet dinner it may be best learned from an experienced, knowledgeable chef, Reiki instruction calls for interaction with a qualified coach, who is available on an ongoing basis, to act as a guide, and to provide a seasoned perspective. Remember: When brief descriptions of various Reiki exercises appear later in this text, these are not meant to instruct! They are included here only as examples of the powerful "beingness" of Reiki. ***One Degree Beyond*** is not a book about "how to"; it is a book about "why to," and the sample exercises are used here to demonstrate benefits. We hope you find them, as we have, especially effective in the release of tension. As such, they are not only tidbits of useful, integrative, reflective Reiki, but can be windows to envisioning how we fit in both a physical and energetic world.

"Oh, what a catastrophe,
what a maiming of love when it was
made personal, merely
personal feeling.
This is what is the matter with us:
we are bleeding at the roots
because we are cut off
from the earth and sun and stars.
Love has become a grinning
mockery because, poor blossom,
we plucked it from its stem
on the Tree of Life
and expected it to
keep on blooming in our civilized
vase on the table."

D.H. Lawrence

The Practice of Reiki

*R*eiki is practiced at home, in the workplace, or whenever or wherever desired, by persons of all ages and degrees of physical fitness. But it is not practiced as one does a religion. Reiki is very definitely *not* a religion. It is:

> • Universal Life-force Energy—as well as that vibrant energy demonstrated by science to exist in and about living creatures,
> *and*
>
> • A *psychophysical methodology* for supporting and/or reordering health mechanisms. It was brought forward by Dr. Mikao Usui. In Reiki practice we may obtain a new charged awareness of our physical and energetic realities; by directly experiencing both *simultaneously,* which can result in shifts in multidimensional mind-body states.

"While exposing his hands... he still guided [them]... with a steady and undisturbed reason,and such presence of mind, as if he had been out of the action and watching it from a distant, passing still from point to point, and assisting...."

Plutarch's Lives

Some Reiki practitioners are very spiritual, some are not. And while Reiki, at some levels, *does* encourage spiritual contemplation (even has a mystic quality) the bottom line is *how* you approach it. In other words, a Reiki practitioner may be a Buddhist, Christian, Jew, Moslem, Hindu or Pagan. This practitioner may be an architect, teacher, doctor, photographer, talent agent, firefighter, novelist, minister, baseball player, web site designer, violinist, accountant, bookkeeper—you get the idea. No one is excluded from learning and practicing Reiki. Age range is not a limitation, nor is sex, body shape or size, talent, intelligence, perceived eccentricities or occupation... but presence of mind is necessary and *Intent is essential.*

Intent

*O*ver the years, I have come to see that from whatever vantage point we view life, it is wise to take into account how pivotal is the roll of *Intent*! Three decades ago IBM researcher, Marcel Vogel, concluded two things about *Intent*:

> • *Intent produces an energy field.*
> • *Our thoughts and emotions affect living things around us.*

Intent is serious business. This takes precedence in the practice of Reiki—what you *intend,* not who you are, or what you look like. *Intent! Intent! Intent!*

Reiki is a standard therapy, used with success in complementary medicine. Worldwide, a broad spectrum of practicing health professionals (hopefully, aware of the importance of *Intent*) employ or recommend it: doctors, dentists, nurses, physical and occupational therapists, ministers, chiropractors, psychologists, massage therapists, barbers and cosmetologists. These people are licensed to do "hands-on" body work and use the Reiki methodology in therapeutic environments for all manner of ailments, including acute and chronic stress. (If you are not a licensed health professional or a minister, you would need to check the laws and certifications in your part of the world before engaging in Reiki as a therapist.)

"I gave him a look,
but no other answer;
and going to my good old master,
said a few words of comfort
and encouragment. He put his
hand upon my shoulder,
as it had been his custom to do
when I was quite a little fellow...."

Charles Dickens
David Copperfield

"Reiki is from the heart."

Mari Hall
Practical Reiki

For those of you who are or will become certified Reiki practitioners and are interested in sharing Reiki sessions with other Reiki initiates, licensing is not required. A good idea is to hook up with a group of friends, family members or other Reiki folk for exchanging Reiki. In our neck of the woods, such gatherings are called "Reiki Circles." Here endless possibility is celebrated—as in the true story which follows:

Reflective Process: *Do the consistent and compassionate attention of the practitioner and the special energy transference sessions make a difference in the story that follows? As you read, make up your own mind. I can say that all of the principals in this tale believe that Reiki made a world of difference. The story is repeated here as an illustration of what we know to be possible.*

The True Story of Ken and Billy

Like many practitioners of Reiki whom I've had the good fortune to meet over the years, Ken was a special guy with a special mission. He wanted to share life's blessings with others. When a group of us got together to discuss the practice of Reiki and to share the experience in the community, you couldn't miss Ken. He was a real standout, and not just because of his appearance --I remember clearly that Ken had the countenance of one who is at peace with himself.

This man was a 277-pound angel, who looked as if he should have been a defensive back for the Seattle Seahawks. For all his size, however, Ken was unassuming and remarkably gentle. As I observed him patiently working with folks who were interested in Reiki therapy, I recall how quickly he would center himself, and how sweet was the expression on his broad face as he did so. I remember quite vividly the night he told our small gathering of a recent commitment he had made, how that face was etched with compassion as he spoke of a small child, Billy who needed assistance. "You see," Ken told us, "Billy was born with a very serious intestinal problem." Billy's parents were torn asunder as they watched their little boy suffer—their two-year-old was not expected to make it to his next birthday. Frightened and frustrated by the apparent inability of traditional medicine to treat his conditon successfully, they were ready to try anything, even alternative or complementary strategies, when their friend Ken visited one night. They filled him in on the situation. Knowing that Ken was a Reiki practioner, they wondered if maybe Reiki therapy could help Billy. When Ken volunteered to assist with Reiki, they said, "Why not? We have everything to gain and nothing to lose."

Ken and Billy's dad worked on the same construction team. On work breaks they discussed the options, the program, and the possible outcomes. Ken explained that it had only been a year since he had completed his initial training in Reiki, and that he was somewhat of a novice, but repeated his offer whatever assistance he could. And so the Reiki sessions were planned and got underway.

Three or four times a week Ken would return from a day of pounding nails, shake the sawdust from his clothes, get cleaned up, slick down his unruly hair, put on one of his plaid flannel shirts (he seemed always to wear flannel shirts) and head on over to visit Billy, usually at the local Children's Hospital, where Billy was a patient. Each time the toddler reached a stage of relaxation in the Reiki therapy sessions, Ken noticed a softening in the tense abdominal area. And Billy smiled. Ken reported that while Billy was not thriving, he felt there were some positive signs of improvement and definite pain relief.

The weeks and months went by. Ken kept us informed regularly, and asked for feedback and advice. He told us how he wished there were something more he could do. The people who came to the Reiki Circle were supportive and "distanced" energy medicine directly to Billy, and remembered him in their hearts each week. Then Ken decided that he was ready to deepen his Reiki practice. He had maintained contact with the Reiki Master who had been his Reiki I Instructor. He had just returned from teaching Reiki abroad— and this student was ready. The timing was perfect. Ken told us that he hoped that his intentions to deepen his practice, in combination with the instruction and attuning process of the Reiki II Training would open up a way for a breakthrough for Billy. Ken's heart and his stamina for this demanding practice were as big as he was.

If Ken was optimistic, this was not the case with Billy's parents, who after months of anguish and trauma and no miracle cures, were stretched to the limits of their endurance. After the rigors of the many invasive medical procedures Billy had experienced (and would need to continue to undergo), they did acknowledge that Billy's Reiki therapy had, at least, provided some relief, had seemed at times as comfortable to him as a warm blanket on a cold night. But relief was far short of a cure.

Billy's doctors and nurses, many of whom at first had been reluctant to deposit their trust in Ken's compassionate ministrations, now were discovering Reiki to be an innovative and supportive technique, one which provided them with a new way of looking at their role in the healing process. Nevertheless, their prognosis for Billy was pretty much the same.

It had been almost a year since Billy's Reiki therapy had begun. During this time, Ken completed his Reiki II Training and continued the regular schedule of sessions with his young client. He reported to our group that he was now "concentrating on higher dimensions, while praying, relaxing and opening to the highest good of all concerned...." Ken asserted that he knew that Billy would improve "without a shadow of a doubt."

Shortly after telling this, however, this gentle soul appeared at the Reiki Circle with tears in his eyes. Billy's condition had worsened! Everyone was stunned and saddened. Later that evening, we met again. We empathized, in unison, and focused our thoughts and our hearts in loving concern for Billy. Knowing that Reiki can produce a "healing crisis," we released our attachment to the outcome and simply expected that "the highest good of all concerned" would present itself.

When just a week later Ken arrived uncharacteristically late at our meeting place, we were filled with apprehension and concern. As he rushed in the door and saw our faces, however, he began to glow. "Billy's OK!" he beamed. "Something changed this week and the doctors say that if he can make it through this month, the prognosis is good!"

That was several years ago, and as of the date of this writing Billy is alive and well. He is now in elementary school, a vivacious child, who knows all about a "special energy," a great big "angel" named Ken, and his friends at the Reiki Circle.

Practitioners

What You Need to Start:

- self discipline
- personal intregrity
- humility
- willingness
- sense of openness
- adventuring disposition
- empathy
- compassion
- self-management aptitude
- ability to focus attention

On the part of the recipient or student, and later, on the part of the practitioners of *The Usui System of Reiki*, the primary requirements are few. This is not to say that they are inconsequential. Self-discipline, personal integrity, humility, willingness, a sense of openness to the unexpected or unique and an adventuring disposition are all important. Above all, empathy is mandatory.

As a practitioner, one must be able to learn the Reiki methodology. Confidence grows as the system is used. The ability to sense subtleties and to intuit appropriate responses is very valuable. Finally, the more balanced an individual is, the more ready to scrutinize "personal negativity" and to move into "personal possibility," the more artful can be the Reiki practice.

As we mature in our process, we expand our perception. We begin seeing situations, events, and even physical properties *in new ways*. The more we aspire to the enterprise of climbing the ladder to refreshed awareness, the greater the chances are that we will perceive what we did not notice before.

Make no mistake: with regard to the aspects of Reiki which pull us in—to relaxing, opening, and celebrating Life, into new realms of perception—the winds of change *stir from within*, to swirl about the uncharted spaces of the multidimensional mind-body universe, where they help to create unfolding new patterns of understanding and conceptual development. These "new patterns" flourish in the supportive atmosphere of our belongingness to other beings and the living world. It behooves the practitioner to be observant in this regard, to be open to what is made manifest.

Reiki in a Comfortable Environment

ℬeing comfortable is a very important prerequisite for the practice of Reiki. One of the first things emphasized by my first Reiki teacher was the necessity for getting ourselves comfortable before beginning a session. "You *must* be positioned *comfortably*, within and without!" she insisted. By way of preparation, this means making mind-body adjustments, loosening-up, and breathing in a rhythmic, relaxed manner before starting your Reiki session. (This applies whether you are a participant or practitioner.) I can still hear my teacher. "Remember," she cautioned, "*the Intent in Reiki is to be a catalyst for Life-force Energy, so you must take the time to set your own agenda aside….*"

Reserving a special time and place for the Reiki session, in which you can enjoy a private, undisturbed, "time-out," aids in the revitalizing process. Finding a setting in which you feel comfortable is important. Again, this matters whether you are alone, as a practitioner, or with another, as a participant/recipient. As an example, when practicing Reiki alone, we try to lie on a soft surface, dim the lights, close the door, and remove constricting items such as shoes, watches, and belts. When Reiki therapists treat others, this comfortable surface is usually a special table, which is deeply cushioned and covered in soft fabric. The table provides the correct height for the practitioner, who is seated, and a steady, comfortable resting place upon which the recipient can recline.

"Do you ask why misery abounds among us? I bid you look into the notion we have formed of ourselves in this Universe, and of our duties and destinies there."

Thomas Carlyle
Carlyle's Complete Works, Book Four

Whether you are approaching Reiki as a method for enhancing relaxation, physical improvement, mental/emotional issues, or for deeper insight, you will want to pay close attention to your breathing. Breathing* is an integral part of your personal environment, so prior to the session, calm your thoughts, get "centered" and consciously breathe deeply, concentrating on exhaling fully then inhaling. Next, seek out a mental connection through imagery, with a place in which you feel at ease and again comfortable.

A comfortable length of time for a relaxation session is generally fifty-five minutes. This, of course, can vary, as time and necessity permit. Indeed, "unruffling your fine feathers" may happen in a brief, empathic touch, or in ten minutes (a Reiki Break). Some very distressing concerns respond to marathon sessions, some to daily attention, others to the briefest of gentle Reiki touches. You will quickly come to see this and to recognize your own comfort level and how a shift in awareness portends delicious benefits for yourself, your family, friends, others, or the global community and Mother Earth.

Reiki practice can be beneficial in varying degrees. You may expect minor miracles, or look for more subtle results. Your individual state-of-mind, your belief systems, your objectives, and how much attention you decide to devote to the methodology will influence what happens. Dedication deepens a Reiki practice and broadens desirable outcomes.

See Appendix B

Benefits of the Practice of Reiki

- Reiki practice produces measurable changes in bodily function.

- Involvement in caring for your needs at many levels.

- Enjoyment of mutual benefits when sharing

- Studies show that Reiki helps to balance and ground its participants.

- Commitment to the practice of Reiki provides time for Reflection

- Within the Reiki practice, it can become easier to "listen" carefully to body wisdom.

- Both problem-solving and flexibility can be by-products of the Reiki practice.

- Tension relief, noticeable relaxation.

- Heightened awareness, and mental clarity.

- "Connections," and emotional growth

- Lowered blood pressure, and resistance to anxiety.

- Insight, abundance, and unexpected blessings.

- Pain reduction and preventative care for long term well-being.

- Modification of "old stuff" behaviors, and openness to the new.

Reiki is a highly personal experience—different for everyone. However, for all, the practice affords a system for self-monitoring, relaxed and deep breathing, reflection, heigthened awareness. It is a system for dissolving patterns of longterm stress.

A Being Practice

*A*s you mature in your process, you may come to have new insights directly related to the *experience* of Reiki. An energetic model is easier to fathom when one has firsthand knowledge of nonlocal (energetic) space through Reiki. New scientific truths of a new consciousness are not so disorienting when one is familiar with the energetic territory.

Reiki is a simple way to get in touch with our at-ONE-ment with a vast energetic universe, where, as Thomas Berry, author and professor at Harvard University points out: "The obvious thing… is that there is an absolute coherence within its total structure and functioning,… (and) we find that this universe is intelligible only in the unity of its being." Reiki practice offers a sense of personal integration into this primary, coherent organic, phenomenon: a functioning universe, a living galaxy, a vibrant cosmos.

Perhaps through our personal experience of Reiki, we may relax into feeling comfortable with becoming (ourselves) agents of change, bringing to the human community a timely transformation of consciousness.

Reiki *is* mysterious!

When we allow ourselves to "sink in" with it, to soothe and refresh ourselves, we discover that it is also very powerful. But this is not power as we might ordinarily define it. This is not the power of exerting control over ourselves or others, but the power of abundant good wishes: the fruits of the fertile fields of empathy, balance, interconnectedness, and a holistic view of the cosmos, and our place in it. What greater benefit could be imagined than to become conscious of this special power? Still, benefits are not *reasons* to do Reiki. *Reasons* could be misconstrued as *goals*. In that case, one could mislead oneself to see the practice of *The Usui System of Reiki* as something at which one *does or does not succeed....* *Au contraire!* Reiki is a ***being*** practice!

Although in all my years as a Reiki Master, I have always seen someone relax with Reiki, sometimes a practioner erroneously will conclude that if a shift or a momentous revelation does not occur quickly or "on schedule," it is because they are doing something wrong. At this point, they may start to doubt the therapist if they are a recipient, or themselves or their management of the methodology. *Do not trap yourself into goal orientation.* Standard advice: always simply *experience* Reiki for its own sake, not because of expectations. The results will come of their own accord.

Folks frequently think that "doing" demands results, so the notion of undertaking something with the intent of simply *being*, where the "right" way and the "right" result are of no concern, can feel unusual. Odd as it may seem, however, *in the practice of Reiki, you will discover that the best way to accomplish anything is to let go of trying to accomplish something.* In fact, in the Reiki session, it is okay to let go of trying to accomplish anything at all! Reiki then is a *being* practice, a present time practice, a mysterious practice, and as such, escapes good/bad, either/or, accomplished/failed, polarized, dualistic thinking, the lock step logic of the old Cartesian-Newtonian worldview. Because of this, it offers plenty of paradoxical potentialities. We have the opportunity to learn, by first-hand experience, that in releasing the ladder of expectation, a way opens for the direction and quality of our lives to emerge—towards wholeness, connectedness and health—in our Reiki journey into energy medicine.

"I was getting ready - but did not know it."

Wanja Twan
Longtime Reiki Master

4

Usui:
A Reiki Journey
Into Energy Medicine

"I organize in order to nurture, balancing being. I seal the
imput of birth with the rhythmic tone of equality.
I am guided by my own power doubled."

Mayan Verse

The Core

Princely memories
swirled 'round in his head
like so many butterflies bound for
Home,
fairly astonishing
his eager mind
with joys of places once known,
kingly realms,
music,
rhythm and poem,
until, with half-smile,
he remembered
his own
heart's center.

Wind-in-the-Feather

Buddha was once asked,
"Are you a god?"
He replied, "No."
"Are you an angel then?"
He said, "No."
"Well, then, what are you?"
"I am awake," he said.

~ Buddhist Teacher

Dr. Usui and the Story of Reiki

Throughout the history of humankind, whispers from ancient cultures hinted at a body of knowledge involving the transfer of energy through touch. Elders said that this knowledge was very powerful. Those who held it, held it closely. These were only a chosen few, handing it on from master to student through the spoken word until, their voices quiet, the body of knowledge became mythical.

Still, echoes from a time past remembering persisted, lending credence to the tales of energy unbounded. Were they myth, or did ancient peoples really "use" certain understandings to energize body, mind, and inner spirit, to encourage wholeness through attuning to life-force? If so, could this knowledge be recovered and shared? This was Mikao Usui's burning question, and it became his all-consuming quest. The account of the manner in which he set about exploring that question leads me to believe that Usui will someday be legendary, for he has a heroic character.

"Heat cannot be separated from fire, or beauty from the Eternal."

Dante

It wasn't all that long ago, not hundreds and hundreds of years ago, but in the late 1800s in Japan, that this man of neither too humble nor too exalted origins and status became known for his contributions to others. Many versions, many viewpoints of his story exist. Yet, in some very fundamental sense they do very little to change the overall view of his character or the archetypal pattern we see in his life's unfolding. As a matter of fact, they possess important features in common, and follow the same thread.

In the traditional Usui story, as narrated by Hawayo Takata,* the teacher who first brought Reiki to the West, as well as in numerous variations, we are shown a cultural hero who followed the dictates of his inner voice to succeed in realizing the truths he had sought to understand for many years. Thus, we come to know Usui as a man not satisfied with surface appearances; one who would strive to embody the truths he had found. Furthermore, this was a man who dedicated his efforts to assisting others along the journey of discovery.

The great adventure of Mikao Usui, a familiar teaching story, is meant to inspire the Reiki student and to offer stepping stones to his vision of a universe in which well-being is a *process*. As such, it can guide those who discover it to heightened awareness.

Dr. Mikao Usui

How fortunate for his students that Mikao Usui had the grace to share the moments of his own formation. His stories, his memories accumulated, memories of a long life dedicated to the pursuit of a burning desire. These stories can be like torchlights to practitioners of a methodology based upon his vigilance.

I cannot emphasize strongly enough my gratitude to this humanitarian whose photograph sits before me as I write. If you were to look deeply into his eyes surely you would discover the lights of dignity, civility, and grace. Here too, resides solid good sense. As I regard this face, I am drawn back to a time in the story of his life when "fate" called his core being into question, by delivering a vivid insight after years of research. It was then that Usui uprooted himself from his planned path, and experienced the first reflections of a dawning light. Perhaps such understanding revealed itself to Usui because he had it within himself to acknowledge and to relate to his own experience, and then to take the steps necessary to move beyond the superficial boundaries of the apparent most of us are so inclined to erect.

Clearly, he could have chosen not to commit his life to the pursuit he envisioned, could have avoided the crucial process of relying on his instincts and his open-mindedness to give direction to his journey through life, but he was a man of integrity and inner strength. So it was that within his "inner hearing," on many levels, that he discovered a new way of relating to life, and shared it. Through the practice he developed as a result, he (and we) could spend numerous lifetimes without exhausting the possibilities—that practice, Reiki, a simple yet powerful transformative gift to humankind.

Usui's gifts to us come as a result of his interactions—his mindfulness, and a particular experience—that transformative experience of the heart, which culminated in a profound awakening.

Good lessons are embodied in his life's story. The truths in these lessons are of a different order from dogma or philosophic statement (they lend themselves more, I think, to the language of poetry), yet they invite an awakening, even an evolution of consciousness towards the liberating, the transcendental truths that arrive from earnest striving.

How did this all begin? According to the traditional story, a student's curiousity ignited a perplexing question for his mentor Usui, which in turn led the good man to become a student... but let me pick up the telling of his story as many before me have.

It was a question of *miracles*, and Dr. Usui *did* believe in them. But others were not so ready to acknowledge the possibility of spontaneous healing. So that day, Usui wondered, "What about those who needed to see with their own eyes? Yes, there were those ancient tales of miraculous energy exchange," he mused, "those wonderous accounts of Jesus and of Buddha, but who has seen such aspects of healing in modern times?" He knew then what he must do. He must climb back in history! He must read all the books he could find and he must scour his own intuition. Indeed, some of those stories of miraculous healings had come to his homeland by way of American physician-missionaries who had flocked to Japan in the wake of Admiral Perry's opening of the country to western trade and influence.

So, that was a starting place, but as his journey continued, he began to realize that obscure, ancient teachings were veiled for a reason. He found that Jesus himself had insisted that those who witnessed His healing miracles remain silent. As He sent forth a leper, now cured, He had said, "See thou, say nothing to any man." (Mark 1:43). But who could keep quiet about this kind of news? Human nature was what it was (and is) and that was what Usui was counting on! Almost two thousand years later, Usui found himself on a frigid trail. Nevertheless, Usui's persistence could thaw the most icy landscape, and he was well aware of the power of commitment.

Usui now turned his attention to the "miracles of healing" attributed to the Buddha. He immersed himself in the study of ancient Chinese scripts of the Buddha's teachings. Buddhism had come to China and Tibet in a lengthy process, he remembered. It had originated in India, where the practice was written and taught hundreds of years before it arrived in China. When the Moslems came into influence in India, Buddhism, its denizens, and most of the ancient teachings were eradicated. While this was going on, the war lords of Tibet, who had no written language, were becoming more powerful. One of these, seeking political strength, decided his language would have to take on written form.

The Chinese, as Usui recalled, had by then adopted Buddhism. In the process, they had procured the services of monks and scribes to translate Indian texts, and were well into the Buddhist practice. So the Tibetan king followed suit. He collected as many of the Buddhists who were fleeing India as he could, and set them up in Tibet. He demanded that they devise a written language and that they translate ancient texts.

One of these texts was the *Lotus Sutra*, in which numerous references were made to the Buddha's healing abilities. Dr. Usui had discovered valuable tidbits of information in the *Lotus Sutra*, and was prepared to glean new information from this ancient text. New perspectives began to shine. Among other things, the *Lotus Sutra* describes the Buddha as "wise and astute, brilliant in dispensing medicines, adept at healing all illnesses." (Quoted from Kumarajiva's Chinese version of the *Lotus Sutra* in Raoul Birnbaum's, *The Healing Buddha*, pg. 18.) This may well have mirrored what Usui would have espoused in his own practice of the healing arts, and surely intrigued him.

By this time, too, as he continued to research, it seems that Usui had advanced in meditation and visualization practices, thereby increasing and deepening his awareness of the subtle energies of the human body and how such practices affect consciousness and can produce states of heightened awareness.

As always, Usui chose not to content himself with the obvious. He concentrated on the core. He wanted to understand the text—inside and out. Mere intellectual understanding did not seem quite enough, what was needed was the actual manifestation of the healing powers alluded to in the text.

Now, in the traditional Usui story, an old Zen abbot arrives on the scene, representing a mentor in Usui's life, someone full of empathy, someone whose face was lit with a perpetual smile, someone with whom an immediate sense of kinship was felt—an admired and trusted confident whom Usui acknowledged as teacher and mentor. Usui could become a student—not a student of someone else, but a student of true Self!

Dr. Usui was a punctilious scholar. Before delving into the text, we might expect that he had gathered substantial research on the history of energy transfer and the "marvelous deeds of God." Let's take a look at what he might have found. Evidence of the use of Touch for physical release and healing had come from all ancient cultures, where Touch or "laying-on-of-hands" was common practice. Touch is mentioned in medical texts dating back to 2600 BC. A systematic set of hand movements over specific areas of the body related to various organs was practiced in ancient times. These, too, were recorded in the annals of early medicine. In the Graeco-Roman civilization, healing with Touch was a function of many temples, and healing "miracles" were recorded on stone tablets, which somehow were preserved and destined to be excavated in modern times. Likewise, the records of the scribes of Egypt chronicled the knowledge of hands-on-healing practices. Those records, in hieroglyphs on temple walls and on papyrus, also revealed that the laying-on of-hands was a customary practice of ancient Egyptian physicians. In India, in traditional Hindu practice, Touch communicated the spiritual union between humans and God, producing a spiritual awakening, great comfort, solace and healing. This awareness of the God-to-human connection was evidenced in the healings attributed to Christ—the very healings Usui had heard about from the missionary-physicians he had studied with. Undoubtedly, they had also contributed to the inspiration which had prodded him into his prolonged search and had ignited his quest for illumination.

Indeed, Touch is a familiar theme in the story of humankind. In tracing the historical role of Touch, we encounter most cultures of the world. The cultures of China, Tibet, India, Japan, Egypt, Europe, Eskimo peoples, Native Americans, the Aborigines of Australia, and various island nations all employed (and still employ) it.

During his years of self-discovery, Dr. Usui began as well to translate material from Sanskrit and Tibetan sources. Because of his steadfast research effort, he had become attuned to nuances in structure and form and eventually found certain passages that led him deeper into himself. He read and reread these, at last fathoming different meanings, different connections within himself and a different way to open himself more... and more... until he was open to receive whatever the Universe would offer him as a gift. "Perhaps, the key to spontaneous healing is an expanded awareness of our physical nature," he may have surmised, and, indeed, after more than a decade in inquiry, Dr. Usui rediscovered an obscure door to ancient understanding.

However, it is one thing to be able to understand how to do something, to fish, to paint, to write—it is entirely another to be able to do what you wish. So a new question arose: If one understands the principles, how then does one allow being to guide self-realization wherever it needs to go in order that healing and "wholing" may spontaneously unfold? And now the story continues....

Usui's mentor, who was as intrigued by this question as was Usui himself, suggested that they ponder what lay ahead. Both men would contemplate and enjoy their silent communication. Enlightened masters had visited possibility, through contemplation for thousands of years. It was expected that following this example, looking deeply within their own nature as human beings, as mindful creatures, as explorers, as passive observers, they might tap the depths of wisdom. In deep reflection lay the gateway to transpersonal reality. Perhaps on this occasion both men sat together quietly and rested in their breathing. Finally Dr. Usui had a clear intuition of what to do: Mt. Kurama beckoned. (Mt. Kurama was then and still is a favorite place for seeking inner vision. It is a natural retreat area available for those engaging in ascetic training which fosters the experience of self in a body of light). He would go on retreat there with the special intent of receiving a direct transmission of the ancient understandings through actualizing the practice itself. Since obviously there was no one living who could transfer this knowledge, he would seek to achieve the empowerments by applying himself wholeheartedly.

Eagerness quelled Usui's fear as he approached the mountain. Anticipation of a clear vision presenting itself urged him on, as he fasted and meditated from a solitary place. Focused on his intent, Usui set out, walking with a purposeful stride from dawn to dusk, carrying with him a goatskin of water and an open heart. As he made his way along the road, a decade of research knocked on the door of Usui's mind. He realized that this was not his mission alone. Others were counting on him. He would remain steadfast, no matter what might happen in the weeks to come, even if his very life were at stake!

Usui took the rigorous climb with zeal. Presently, he came to a quiet spot, with a single pine tree and an unhindered view, into which a stream flowed. He selected twenty-one stones, then seated himself for meditation; there began the ritual of the twenty-one day fast, as he placed the stones about him. These stones, he would cast aside, one at a time, each day, at dawn.

The days passed, uneventfully, one by one. The shadows of dawn and dusk moved across the mountainside as the sun rose and set. And so it was, that the days wore on, and the stones disappeared in six directions, until only one remained.

Fasting and meditation are, and have been, used by those seeking enlightenment since time immemorial. Contemporary scientific documentation supports what the wise ones of old knew all along: brain chemistry changes when subjects fast, or meditate, releasing consciousness-enhancing substances. Furthermore, the focusing of attention that occurs in meditation or deep contemplation seems to organize left-right brain activity into coherent, interacting patterns. This can result in profound awareness, mystical experiences, and a cosmic sense of reality. When the veils of earthly illusion lift, essence shines forth. This is what Usui, alone on the Sacred Mountain, having prepared for this understanding (exhaustively) expected. He awaited a unitive experience.

Usui's resolve reminds us of the Buddha who sat under the Bodhi tree, determined not to rise until enlightenment was won. Usui went to the mountain to actualize teachings that would unlock the mysteries of the power of spirituality to heal body and mind, and to find balance in the wholesomeness of *Universal Life-force Energy.*

There is a precedent set in the spiritual tradition of several cultures that it takes twenty-one days to change consciousness. This particular symmetry honors the noteworthy achievement of a remarkable man. We have hinted at the archetypal nature of Usui's journey. May this inspire us to complete our own quest for resonance with Life-force Energy.

The dawning of the twenty-first day was very dark. It found Mikao Usui in a trance, with one stone still in its resting spot before him. Then, from the far reaches of his consciousness, there emerged in the still dark sky, a radiant, intense light, piercing the heavens, searing toward him!

"This is a test," he exclaimed, "I will face it!"

With eyes open wide, he sat still as the light blazed toward him with dazzling brilliance. It did not relent! Swiftly, it struck him between the eyes.

Then slowly, a vision began to unfold: a vision of millions of colors and rainbows, and iridescent bubbles dancing before him, filling the sky with red, moving from right to left, changing from orange and yellow, to green, and blue, and purple. The whole sky was now a rainbow! And there was more. As he gazed at the phenomenon, shimmering glyphs, representing the actualization of the truth and empowerment inherent in ancient texts followed one another onto the magnificent canopy above and presented themselves before him.

At once he knew, in the deepest part of his humanity, what they were for, how to use them, and that they came from a place of pure joy within himself. And as he returned to this reality of time and place—to Mount Kurama—he knew that his vision had manifested a transformation of consciousness.

To Be Continued In First Degree Training

...Crimson gleams of matter
gliding imperceptibly
Into the gold of spirit,
Ultimately to become
Transformed
Into the incandescence
of a Universe
That is a Person...

And through all this,
There blows,
Animating it,
And spreading over it
a fragrant balm,
A Zephyr of Union.

Pierre Teilhard de Chardin

5

One Degree Beyond

"When the mind stays serene, whatever happens to us is good."

Rainer Maria Rilke

The Cosmic Circle

Then chiefs
and sons of chiefs
upon the waters did reflect,

while one who told the story
of the People's singing,
dancing 'round the sacred tree,
remembered...
and with prayer stick,
to the world of Spirit went,
wherein there is no time.

Here, drinking from eternal waters,
knowing, giving thanks,
the wise one
flung the stick to Stream,

"I see the Spirit of the Earth
in each cosmic circle unfolding,
from smallest to grand,
from family, and tribes
to nations, and lands,
blossoming forth from EarthMother
spiraling, celebrating,
from deep within the Mustard Seed," she sang.

And chiefs, and sons of chiefs
in hope and harmony
upon the waters did reflect.

Wind-in-the-Feather

On this dusty road
A turtle's crossing is cause
For celebration!

~ Scott Christopher

One Degree Beyond
Those Influences, Those Paths

It is interesting how things transpire in our lives. Have you ever noticed how you get what you need when you need it? So it was with Usui, and so it has been with me, and probably you! I beg your indulgence now as I take you back once more to "fortuitous detours" and a road which led me to connect more closely to Reiki. Although my discovery was but a butterfly's kiss compared to that of Usui, its unique quality and its beneficial aftermath cannot be denied.

As you will recall, my original search was for a fresh approach to relaxing in a competitive, intense environment. I wanted to know how to mitigate the effects of stress for myself —and for my corporate clients. My adventures in Arizona inspired me to pursue further Reiki experiences and eventually resulted in my enrolling in a Reiki Training program. I decided that "what I needed" next was some more formal training in stress reduction methodology. Signposts had led me to a weekend Reiki seminar on Orcas Island in the state of Washington. I can remember thinking at the time that once again, here I was, "getting what I needed." What I expected, therefore, was to learn some practical hands-on, sure-fire techniques that I could take back and try on my co-workers. What I got, and what it is very clear to me now I really needed, was the gift of an individual like Mikao Usui! Quite frankly, I may not have even noticed him at this weekend seminar, had I not been open to *seeing things in a new way.*

There on Orcas Island, as our teacher wove Usui's tale in the great oral tradition, it was easy to connect with his persistent search and integrity in a visceral way. The story impressed me. As I "listened" with a new found inner hearing, the story confirmed something about intent for me, and helped me to solidify my understanding of Reiki as both a methodology and as an artform which held *promise*. Thus, I came to see Usui's story as a *model* for a singular way of relating to life.

Later, returning by ferry to Friday Harbor, strains of Dr. Usui's story stayed with me, creating a pensive mood despite rolling seas. I began to see deeper meanings in the story. Winter winds whipped up irregular swells (and green-faced passengers) as we plied our way between islands, but as a result of my earlier experiences, my senses were heightened and even seemed to be fed by the intermittent squalls. Usui's story had stirred something deep within, and I wasn't willing to let go of that feeling. What I wanted now was to find something concrete, a physical sign, to anchor me to a powerful set of experiences. On our walk later that evening, I promised myself that Maggie (the ever-willing) and I would search for this anchor, and that's just what we did.

Mementos Borne of Spirit

The elements combined to design a setting that had all our senses on alert. Maggie's fur bristled. I was vividly aware of my surroundings. Mists with a timeless quality shrouded the Island in a fluctuating and luminous cloak. Sea sounds and fog horns lent their voices to a mysterious ghostly chorus. Ocean sprays salted the air and flavored it while clouds loomed low on the horizon. As the full moon finally broke through to light the way (and cast shadows all about us), *my* hair was bristling! Here we were at South Beach, one of our favorite haunts, and on such a lonely night, I sensed that somehow we were not alone. It was in fact delightfully spooky, a fine place in which my imagination could play, unselfconsciously.

A century ago, the native Haida Tribes folk had canoed across the waters of the Straits of San Juan de Fuca, unafraid of the will of the rough currents. They had carried their sick to South Beach to be healed. Most of us had heard about the arrival of their canoes from old timers on the Island. South Beach, "The Sacred Healing Place," I mused, absorbing the misty landscape of rocks and logs and dark waters beyond. Neither herring ball nor fishing boat made its presence known on the seas that night. "If anyone is watching, of what interest could be two pals, merging into a surrealistic landscape, painted on the edge of the world and time," I thought to myself, enjoying the drama.

During the day, South Beach is stunning. It is part of a National Historical Park, once the station of a regiment of American soldiers deployed here in the late 1800s to protect U.S. interests during a territory dispute with our neighbors to the north. Wide expanses, formerly cleared for parade grounds, are now home to a variety of bunnies, who pop in-and-out of their warrens, where the land reaches down to the sea, buttressed by enormous granite boulders. Not a single tree decorates the area; only grasses, in perpetual motion.

By contrast, on a winter night, with mists, sea sounds, and moonlight, South Beach is startling, even mystical!

Maggie and I established an observation post by a huge, damp, old knotty log, washed up long ago at the foot of the towering granite outcroppings. In the summer these logs were smooth and warm as giant goddess-shoulders, but tonight they appeared rough and silent, beached sea-creatures—Poseidon's outcasts.

"This *is* spooky!" I shivered. Instantly, I thought of how courageous Usui had been, sitting all alone on a mountain with all kinds of real hazards and no food for three weeks; and I wondered how I'd withstand such a test, if mere shadows and mists could affect me so. I cast a furtive look about, half expecting to see the apparition of some Haida chief. In this atmosphere, who knew what might show up? In my heart, I wished for a memento borne of spirit as I cast another sidelong glance down the beach. And that's when I saw it. A shiny object near the log caught my eye in the moonlight.

"What's this?!" I exclaimed, as I followed the glint, and with anxious fingers extracted a silver disc from the rocks. It was a charm, probably lost from the bracelet of one of last summer's tourists. (No, no it really hadn't materialized!) As an equally curious Maggie prodded me with her wet nose, I held the disc up and the moonlight captured it again. There, in bas relief, were mounted hands, holding a heart. The symbology could not escape me. I was immediately reminded of Usui, the strong-hearted man, whose generous spirit still touches so many. I tucked the charm anchor in my glove, delighted.

And so it is, that that night, that "cosmic gift" is not just a memory of some other moment, but lives with me today. That small silver piece has become my focusing point, reminding me of what I believe Mikao Usui has come to represent: Openness, Celebration, and Pure Heart Energy, in a Reiki journey just one degree beyond the apparent.

Reflection

*O*ver the years, I've come to see that pausing to reflect upon our chance happenings, as I did that night at South Beach many years ago, has a way of putting things into perspective. Perhaps finding your own connection with Usui's journey into energy medicine will benefit you as it did me. Perhaps some other connection will be your way. Regardless, taking the time to look for meaning and import at signpost opportunities, if you are open to the message, can lead you to a significantly new and exciting way of perceiving and acting in the universe.

In a world on the brink of awakening to a new understanding of multidimensional reality, of a whole systems cosmology, all too often we do not permit ourselves the leisure of letting in and savoring our experiences; we do not treat ourselves to the luxury of being open to signs and pathways. If we do so treat ourselves, is it not possible that we are a mere few steps away from " follow[ing] our bliss" as suggested by Joseph Campbell? Usui's story, and indeed on a lesser scale perhaps, my story, are reminders (including *your* stories) that *it is possible to do this*. What can happen when we do?

"Reflection:
the transition (which is like a second birth) from simple life to 'Life Squared.'"

Pierre Teilhard de Chardin

❖

Contemplation can disclose the subtle, the sublime, the sacred, the profane when we reflect as a student of Life by asking: "What can I learn from this?" This question implies a trusting in the life *process*. If we are paying attention, Life may reveal it's secrets. In some small way I like to think that this is what happened for Suzanne, a student in my very first Reiki Training class.

Suzanne's Story: My First Encounter with Usui

"*A* painful stumbling block for me, as I entered the world of Reiki, was that this ancient healing practice was rediscovered by a *man*, and that men dominated the field of healing in Japan. Mikao Usui is our teacher's hero. I had no heroes, no male mentors. I realize with sorrow that I really didn't like men. As a woman highly conscious of a second-class citizen status, I had always felt shame, resentment, and frequently anger around men. Resentment that I was not a man with a man's privileges, shame that men wanted me physically but seemed to have no interest in me as a person, anger that they could not honor my intelligence. Used by men, abused by men. And yet, married to a man and calling him best friend. Confused? Yes. Sick and aching? You bet. Could this be a major blockage to my healing, this overwhelming negativity towards half of the human race? Why, yes, I think it fair to say that this was something big for me. Sad....

"I think these thoughts as I sit on the beach with my sister. The waves move in and out. I look down, there by my shoe is a small tear-shaped, grey stone. I hold it in my hand and Usui says to me, 'Cry no more. Hold your tears in your hands and let your eyes see goodness in man.'

"I have found my Reiki totem, the hard rocky tear of years of betrayal— my sorrow, rock hard, unyielding, a stone behind my eye, a boulder on my shoulder (now transformed), in Usui's words of healing."

Try This Process: Step One
Being With Usui For 21 Days

For the next 21 days reflect upon Usui's story. Put yourself in the story. Contemplate it carefully, but do not worry if the story and your experience are not the same (in fact, I can guarantee you—they will NEVER be the same). Just see what happens—experience it. Make an effort to note your discoveries and thoughts in some tangible way.

Day	Reflection	
1	Can energy *really* be exchanged? If this is so, how can it be?	
2	Does the effort of exchanging energy have its rewards? Drawbacks? What are they?	
3	What challenges *your* honesty?	
4	What challenges *your* personal integrity?	
5	If *you* operate apart from your personal, mental, emotional comfort zones, what challenging factors present themselves?	
6	How do *you* react to the long and short term pressure of exploring just one degree beyond the apparent?	
7	As you "look within"—become a student of *Yourself*—and of yourself in context.	
8	When was the last time *you* sojourned alone?	
9	When was the last time *you* climbed a difficult "sacred mountain?"	
10	How far are *you* willing to go, to honor *your* inner-spirit?	
11	How do you view your energetic and physical dynamic?	
12	What is the value of friendship to *you*?	
13	What part does sharing thoughts play in *your* creative process?	
14	For you, how doable is a three-week "vision quest?"	
15	How does the model of listening with your "inner hearing" and seeing with "inner vision" relate to *you*?	
16	How may you prepare, as did Usui, to "manifest a transformation of consciousness?"	
17	Within the context of an awakened realization of your dual (physical/energetic) citizenship, how would you define "distress?"	
18	What was it in Usui's makeup that allowed him to forge ahead with his explorations?	
19	How does this relate to *you*?	
20	If Usui were alive today how would he see the big picture?	
21	If Mikao Usui had something to say to *you*, what would it be?	

Try This Process: Step Two
Using the Story of Usui as a Model

For the next 21 days consider Usui's story as it relates to your life. Set aside morning and evening contemplation time and space. Note insights in a special journal, writing a minimum of two pages each day by using the "signposts" on this page as prompters as you progress.

Signposts

◈ Dedication, "Giri"
Day 1

◈ Mentors and Mentoring
Day 8

◈ Enlightened Understanding
Day 15

◈ The Power of Commitment
Day 2

◈ Always Possibility
Day 9

◈ Place of Pure Joy
Day 16

◈ Willing to Put in the Effort
Day 3

◈ Fathoming Different Meanings
Day 10

◈ Manifest a Transformation
Day 17

◈ Worthy of Respect
Day 4

◈ Student of Self
Day 11

◈ Ancient Wisdom
Day 18

◈ Determination, Patience
Day 5

◈ Trusting the Process
Day 12

◈ New "Ladders"
Day 19

◈ When You Least Expect It
Day 6

◈ Pure Potential
Day 13

◈ Beyond the Apparent
Day 20

◈ Look Deeply, Intuit, Explore
Day 7

◈ Focused Attention
Day 14

◈ Awakening
Day 21

Try This Process: Step Three
Summarizing the Reflections

At the end of your 21-day journey, please summarize the implications the past 21 days of reflection have manifested.

- *Your Burning Question(s):*

- *Physical/Nonphysical Needs:*

- *Challenges:*

- *Perspectives:*

- *Insights/Sharing:*

- *Developmental Possibilities:*

- *Personal Integrity:*

- *Global Healing:*

6

Keys to an Unfolding Process

"My desire for knowledge is intermittent; but my desire to commune with the spirit of the universe, to be intoxicated with the fumes, call it, of divine nectar, to bear my head through atmospheres, and over heights unknown to my feet, is perennial and constant."

Henry David Thoreau

Tapestry

She looked in the mirror,
And saw behind her
A tapestry
Of sunlight 'midst dancing leaves
Stirred by the breeze
Gently.

And trees, now in full leaf,
Who only yesterday displayed Spring
buds,
And but the day before crackled in
Winter's blow.

She looked in the mirror,
And saw before her
The reflection
In her mind's eye, of dancing leaves,
Stirred by the breeze
Gently.

And knew, all at once, the mirror was
her mind,
The winds of change
But players on it.

Wind-in-the-Feather

*"Finally let us not forget that we are in a continuous
relationship with ourselves."*

~ Peter Russell
The White Hole in Time

Collective Soul

*F*or twenty years I have worked with a wide range of
people in this country and abroad, and I think it is fair to
say that of the hundreds of people I have met in my journey
into *energy medicine*, none have taught me more than my
own students. These self-possessed individuals, who try
hard to live up to certain firmly held principles in the practice
of Reiki, who have a sense of humor about themselves and
a keen eye for the inclinations of others, and who are ever
mindful of the changing seasons of our lives—in the pregnant
moments of Earth Mother—in the empty fullness which
leads to liberation —and in the message, "we must not be
selfish, we must share with others," likewise have shared
with me a collective vision.

"The only matter not agreed upon
was this, that the Senate and Counsuls
rested their hopes on nothing else
than on arms; the plebeians preferred
anything to war."

Titus Livius
The History of Rome

Our Essence is Energy

"Energetic resonance is not an 'all or none' process: a system resonates in response to a range of frequencies which are more or less close to its natural frequency...."

Rupert Sheldrake
A New Science of Life

*O*ur essence is energy. Just as much as we are creatures of a physical nature, we are in that measure creatures of an energetic realm. We are thinking, transcending, transforming beings, distinct as whirlpools in a stream, yet one with the stream. Or at least, that is what the scientific facts indicate.

New thought is based on the sophisticated awareness of the potentiality of an imminent and major transformation of consciousness regarding how we come to view the *relational aspects* of our experience. A fundamental, dynamic aspect in our physical surroundings can be seen easily in chemistry experiments in which—given just the right combinations of pressure, temperature, proportion and so forth, and with the right catalyst—matter transforms itself from one state to another. This is a reflection of a wider picture. Unity in diversity manifests itself at the higher levels of the dynamic, where interconnectedness, interrelatedness, and other key energy transactions demonstrate that this process follows a pattern and a direction (albeit spiced with mysterious discontinuities.)

So we may venture that universal destiny is written in all that is seen, or is not visible. It is written in "a code of energetics" for the bold explorer to decipher. Beyond the literal is an analogical interpretation, which may open to an ultimate, spiritual, even mystical sense of our place in the vastness of creation.

Where does Reiki (the practice) fit in all of this? How is Reiki (the *experience*) both a direct connection with the physical, *and* an experience of an energetic reality?

Before we go into this discussion, we need to reflect upon the notion that the universe is one, indivisible, dynamic whole. It is best understood in terms of *relationships* and *integration*. In the mechanistic view, the earth is a composite of discrete parts. Now we are coming to see that the living global community is in systemic synergy—woven, as it were, in a cosmic web which is intrinsically dynamic.

The significance of the practice of Reiki within this context stems from its power to awaken those deep knowings which feed this important understanding. Knowledge of the facets of the Reiki jewel are illuminated within a process which many say finds its fulfillment in celebrating a new vision of life....In the following pages, we reflect upon such matters, preparing ourselves for a journey into the heart of a reality that is like a sea of sparkling generative power ... just one degree beyond the apparent.

Moving Into an Energetic Reality

In every phase of our emotional, aesthetic, and imaginative lives, we are dependent on our perceptions of the world about us. We frame an understanding through conceptualization. With regard to the practice of Reiki, for instance, we observe that the conceptual framework is one of balance, detachment from ego, and holism. This framework is given definition by the integrity of order built-in to *life-process.* These are the main concepts which provide a structure through which we can balance, nurture, and refine our consciousness of a "new way" of viewing the universe. Again, as we reflect upon it, we see that these concepts express themselves in the Reiki practice which can become for us a gateway—a *direct experience* of an energetic reality.

One discovers a great deal as one moves into the practice of Reiki. For one attuned, there is much to be unveiled as the months and years go by, as mystery becomes mysteriously more mysterious and the artscience unfolds. Between the challenge of discovery and the unknown lies an opportunity for deeper understanding.

"Our task must be
to free ourselves…
by widening our circle
of compassion
to embrace all living beings
and all of nature."

Albert Einstein

For those who brave the exploration, clues to the experience of a vast, dynamic, unfolding universe appear as, through the practice of Reiki, we commence to expand our universe of discourse. With a new "inner hearing" and an energized "inner sight" we can begin to envision a deeper harmony—a coherent Whole—and within this Whole, our integral relationship to It. But lest we float into the ethers reminding our friends of so many "airy-fairies," let me share a story that will put this all in perspective....

Live Life with Passion and Charisma

In the years before a back road trip led me to discover Reiki, the bulk of my management consulting practice involved give-and-take with high-performance, get-it-out-there, results-oriented fast-trackers in marketing-communications-sales. Things were hyphenated-to-the-max around these "win-win" stars, who coped with (or tried to cope with) the pressures accompanying their status. There were those notable few, however, who *always seemed calm.* They seemed to structure their day to allow time for *relaxation.* Everyone relished working with these people. They were leaders with high energy who appeared to derive their comfort not from aggressive competition, but from *creative action.* Funny thing; somehow they got the message across that *they* knew, that they *knew*, their successes derived from a combination of willingness to recognize and move *with* opportunity, and the spirit of thrill and joy in life that they embraced. Their message: *"Live Life with Passion and Charisma!"*

Here follows the story of one of these bright lights.

"The only thing you have to offer to another being, ever, is your own state of being."

Ram Dass

Perceive the World as if You were a Child

*N*orm had always said, "Perceive the world as if you were a child." He had the slogan printed in bold italics on memo pads that he handed out to his sales team. It was plastered on the office walls. It was above his door, even on the border surrounding his license plate! It may have seemed a bit odd (if you didn't know Norm) for a guy with an advanced degree in electrical engineering to be so taken with this motto, but it made perfect sense to his staff and to me.

Norm was the manager of one of the "Big Three" automotive accounts for a premier manufacturer of computers. This company (and Norm) hired a good number of senior marketing types through our search firm, so I got to know him pretty well over a period of about fifteen years.

Norm had an uncanny understanding of what was being said between the lines, of what comprised a hidden agenda, of moving targets, of consideration, and of uncompromising common sense. He applied his wisdom in the field of business, but he learned it in another kind of field.

Norm understood how to tune-into the *energies* of Nature. This "added dimension" he employed to the benefit of all in a business environment, and perpetuated as a gift-of-the-spirit to his family and friends, by helping us align with the energetics of the natural cycles of the seasons. At any time of the year this curious pathfinder might be planning a pilgrimage --like the one he organized after the Summer of the Twisters.

Norm had been out assessing the storm damage on the family property shortly after a tornado had ripped through, felling a stand of birch. Norm saw this as an opportunity. He got his sons and wife interested and then the whole family harvested the bark, and engineered and then crafted a canoe which accommodated four people, a dog, supplies, and fishing gear. They were reinventing a time-honored family tradition, readying themselves for a "sacred pilgrimage" into the back canals and marshlands of Harsen's Island, a wildlife refuge bordering Lake St. Clair, the smallest of the Great Lakes.

Without mishap, in the predawn hours, maintaining near silence, Norm and the family launched their craft, pushed off with their paddles, and slipped into the fog, imperceptibly. They were paddling their way to a rendezvous with some small mouth bass, and the spirits of the ancestors of the "Grasses Place." Norm's great-grandfather, a Huron, had fished where the reeds and cattails waved. Generations later, Norm knew the exact spot where the Old Man had fished, but not by the grasses alone. He could *feel* it. "What makes a place special is the *energy*," he insisted. What Norm was describing was how what some folks call influences, emissions, insights, intuitive knowings, openings, or celebrations bring forth *an alignment with an essential resonance within the universe*. Norm recognized the ceaseless patterns of change within a framework of order.

Part of the beauty of the practice of Reiki, just as in Norm's "sacred pilgrimage," lies in the process of teaching ourselves higher skills, by which we arrive at a place of inner truth. In Reiki, we are both training our mind to stay focused (because it is grounded by a physical task), and moving one degree beyond the obvious to tune-in to a system of energetics. But, let's let Norm pick up this discussion.

❦ The Smirbs ❦

One day when Norm and his eldest son were having lunch at a local drive-in restaurant, Norm got to talking about how "perceiving the world as if you were a child" dovetailed with his personal theories of quantum mechanical physics. Norm always spoke softly when he had some bit of wisdom to share, and he had a habit of starting important lessons with "Well, let's see...."

"Well, let's see," Norm proffered to his son, as they concluded a thoughtful talk about their canoe trip to the Old One's fishing grounds. "Well, let's see... you asked me about how I got to know that place by its *energy*..." and Norm's voice deepened with the confidence he was about to share. "Son," he nodded, "the first thing you need to know is to *pay attention* to each place you go." He explained how each place, even the root beer stand where they were that minute, had its own "aura." Then he continued, "and then you have to be able to *see yourself* as having that same kind of energy, even though it's not physical."

"Can you do that?", he asked, as his son nodded affirmatively. "If you can," he continued, "then you can also see that you are *both solid and three dimensional and beyond time and place.*"

Seeing his son's eyebrows knit together, Norm reminded him how water could have the properties of a solid, liquid and gas, and that we are like that except we are solid and energy all at one time. Without hesitating, Norm reached for a large recycled napkin from the tray attached to the window, unclipped his pen from his shirt pocket, and began doodling the way he was apt to do...while his son peered over an order of french fries.

"Well, let's see...," Norm murmured, "Well, let's see...there were these two funny little guys called "Smirbs" (which stands for small-time energy beings), one day as they were just *being* where they were, an energy ball happened to bounce into their playspace." (Norm was drawing cartoon characters observing a round object which was going "boing.")

Norm raised his left eyebrow. "Smirb One *(S1)* grabbed the ball, and *zoooom*...before he really thought about it, he was showing off, whirling it around his head until it took off on its own!" Norm's pen was flying now as he scratched out the next scene in short, rapid strokes. "Well, let's see... you guessed it , that ball was out of control...it went boinging back and forth all over the place with *S1* in mad pursuit until it boinged right into *S2's* large nose. It wasn't on purpose or anything, just 'cuz *S1* was an apprentice energy being." Norm's face now expanded in a wide grin as he chuckled out loud and looked down at the cartoon Smirbs, and over at his son. "Do you know what happened next?" he asked. "Well, things got out of hand; there was a chain reaction and *S2*, snagging the ball and hurling it right back at *S1's* nose...entirely forgetting: *Everything is by nature interconnected, if you hurt somebody else, you're really hurting yourself.*"

His son nodded, drinking the last of his soda, but kept quiet. He knew his dad still had something on his mind. And he was right. "Well, let's see...Hmmm," Norm said gravely... "what if *S1* = Earthlings, and *S2* = Mother Earth!? *What would happen to Mother Earth if S1 forgot The First Law of Multidimensional Energetics, that everything is by nature interconnected?*

Norm's Napkin

"Well, let's see...Hmmm," Norm said gravely... "what if S1, = Earthlings and S2 = Mother Earth? What would happen to Mother Earth if S1 forgot The First Law of Multidimensional Energetics, that everything is by nature interconnected? Ouch!"

Try This Process:
The Smirbs

Journal

- *Begin observing yourself in nature.*

- *Go to a natural area near where you live and see if you can get a "sense of place" - a sense of being attracted to a particular spot.*

- *Consider Norm's story of the "Smirbs."*

- *What is the moral of that story?*

- *Note your response(s).*

Try This Process:
Sacred Pilgrimage

- *Plan a "sacred pilgrimage" to Egypt (even if it is just in your imagination).*

- *When you find yourself at the foot of the Great Pyramid, what are your feelings, on multidimensional levels? Note your response.*

- *How is this response aligned with Norm's observation? "What makes a place special is the energy."*

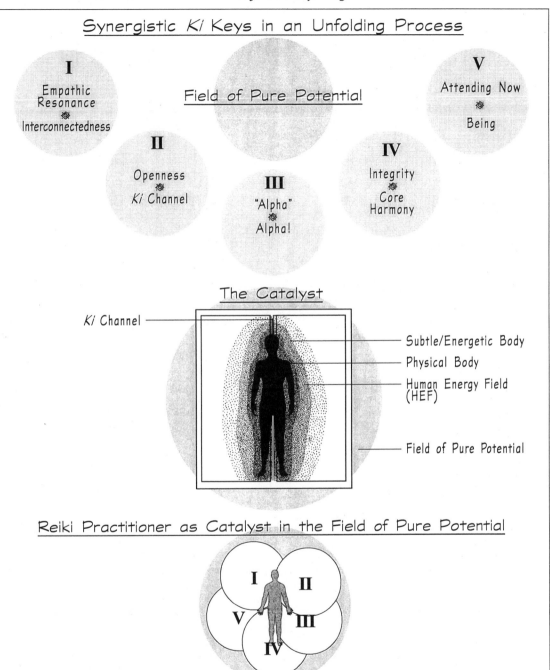

Synergistic *Ki* Keys in an Unfolding Process

I
Empathic Resonance
Interconnectedness

Field of Pure Potential

V
Attending Now
Being

II
Openness
Ki Channel

III
"Alpha"
Alpha!

IV
Integrity
Core Harmony

The Catalyst

Ki Channel

Subtle/Energetic Body
Physical Body
Human Energy Field (HEF)

Field of Pure Potential

Reiki Practitioner as Catalyst in the Field of Pure Potential

I   II   V   III   IV

7

Empathic Resonance, and Interconnectedness

"There is a fantastic spectacle staring us in the face, of a rapidly rising collective reflection, moving in step with and increasingly unitary organization."

Pierre Teilhard de Chardin

Light of the Inner Garden

Look at the butterfly
Fumbling from cocoon
Easing into a renaissance
Of color, and of light; swooning;
Freeing essence
From the night.

O Being of profound integration,
O hallowed one, O celebration,
Tranquility;
Integrity, drifting into flight,
You are the silent flutter
Of profound insight.

Wind-in-the-Feather

Experiencing Energetics
Synergistic *Ki* Keys in an Unfolding Process

I. Empathic Resonance and Interconnectedness

II. Openness and the *Ki* Channel

III. "Alpha" and Alpha!

IV. Integrity and Core Harmony

V. Attending Now and Being

Agents of Change in the Field of Pure Potential

*N*orm would have liked the practice of Reiki. He would have relished the grand opportunity to understand ourselves anew—as beings both physical and energetic—and the possibility within this practice of making a contribution to the living community for "the good of all concerned." How encouraging to discover that the Reiki *experience* activates natural harmonizing skills! These capacities are agents of change.

Let's dub these agents of change, these distinguished energies, the *"Ki" Keys* of the Reiki practice. They strike me as being both door openers (keys) and expressions of life-force energy *(Ki)*, catalysts abiding in a field of pure potential. Each person who *experiences* Reiki is apt to use different images or words to describe the *experience*. The *Ki Keys* are just my way of illustrating this. They are not a part of the Reiki Training, simply reference points in fluid spaces of a new awareness of *being*, vantage points from which to view one's self within a whole system.

I. Empathic Resonance, a *Ki* Key

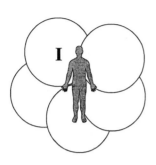

*7*he dictionary defines *empathy* as "identification with or vicarious experiencing of the feelings or thoughts of another." *Resonance* is "the state or quality of being resonant." "*Empathic Resonance*" is a term I coined some years ago to describe what happens when you "tune-in" to another living being, or what happens when you do the same for yourself. This special connection, which is nonphysical, can be just as important as a physical intervention and indeed can affect the physical. It operates on the same principle as belief, which can be powered by any number of thoughts or emotions.

"To change the modality we must change the metaphor."

Jean Houston

All living creatures appear to exhibit empathic resonance. This observation is supported by the research of Eldon Byrd, who was a senior member of the Institute for Electrical and Electronic Engineers, (with a Master's degree in medical engineering and background as an operations analyst with the Advanced Planning and Analysis staff of the Naval Ordinance Laboratory in Maryland). Because he was uniquely qualified, Byrd had laboratory access to highly sensitive, top of the line charting equipment. He was able to demonstrate (as described by Peter Tompkins in his book, *The Secret Life of Plants*) that plants "exhibit a quality of awareness and empathy to other organisms that are stimulated in their presence."* Byrd attributed this awareness in part to "mysterious mechanics of 'bioplasma'" *(Ki)*. He noticed a "*change of biopotential* of the cells from outside to inside membrane,..." *(my italics)*, and said, "mutual communication and empathy is the **key**!" *(his bold)*. If Byrd's research suggests that living creatures exhibit empathic resonance, a more familiar case demonstrates the viability of this energetic exchange.

---

* See "Suggested Reading" Appendix C

Let's take a look at the life experience of Dr. Norman Cousins, which exemplifies empathic communication and indicates that resonating in a healthy way with others is good for us! Dr. Cousins, a medical doctor and later a bestselling author, while in his prime was diagnosed with cancer. He was given just months to live. Refusing standard medical treatment he set out on a program of diet, exercise, and *empathic resonance*. How did he do this?—simply by engrossing himself in funny old movies. Laurel and Hardy and a host of other lighthearted comedians just got him "rolling on the floor," laughing as he watched their screen antics for hours each day. In that empathic exchange, brain and body chemistry altered creating a healing "elixir," positive change, and revitalization of Dr. Cousin's immune system. He recovered, and lived, cancer-free, to share his findings; he died at the age of 76, twenty years later. "Belief becomes biology," he said. Energetic ties certainly exist between living creatures in a natural whole system. They ride on the back of empathy. Now let's take a closer look at this energetic phenomenon.

"Belief becomes biology."

Norman Cousins, M.D.

Empathy is the projection of one's own sense of being, and one's own persona onto that of another in order to understand the other better, and to share the other's experience. "Empathy...is not [just] vicarious experience, for it rises from the depth world, and in its most developed form, from our relationship with the Beloved," writes Jean Houston in *Godseed*.* "Only through empathy is it possible to step into another's shoes without displacing him or her, or losing

"The key to understanding compassion is to enter into a consciousness of interdependence which is a consciousness of equality of being."

Matthew Fox

---

*See "Suggested Reading" Appendix C

one's own identity. (Empathy) releases and empowers the other to become who or what he or she truly is...and thus transformation, be it miracles, healings or new knowledge, can occur. As seen in the case of Dr. Cousins, *"'anything' becomes possible."*

"The individual is universal, and the universal is individual...individuality is only possible if it unfolds from wholeness."

David Bohm

"It takes two to know one."

Gregory Bateson

Empathy is a "gatekeeper" of our *interconnectedness* with all living things. Nowhere is this easier to observe than in the practice of Reiki. Here (just as it happens in the world at large) an infinity of inter-level relations and interactions may occur. But the exchange is firsthand and facilitates the recognition that we do not exist independently of our physical/energetic environment; we both influence and are influenced by it. As bestselling author Matthew Fox states: "The more deeply one sinks into our cosmic existence, the more fully one realizes the truth that there does not exist an inside and an outside cosmos, but rather one cosmos: we are in the cosmos and the cosmos is in us."* Various energetic relationships within a resonating energy field express themselves in the *being* artscience of Reiki. These exchanges can have a substantive, deep and soothing effect, at many, multidimensional levels of *being*. Thus, the practice of Reiki can be a way to make a beginning toward opening "inner knowing." It can be a way to evoke balance and a renewed zest for life on all levels. It can be the avenue to healing connections.

See "Suggested Reading" Appendix C

Synergistic Connections

Over the years, I have come to see how each person with whom I have interacted and empathized in my ongoing practice of Reiki is for me a unique portal to all humanity. I have come to see that each of us is an expression of the Whole of Humanity, and contains the Whole. More and more, I realize that which *is* comes from an Order in which *"everything"* is folded into *Everything*, and, in the most fundamental sense, each of us is *interconnected* with the Whole, and to all others. What of this interconnectedness?

"You don't stop
at your skin."

Dolores Krieger, Ph.D., R.N.

In the past half century, astrophysical, quantum mechanical, astronomical, and biological theorists, among others, have been exploring the concept and evidence of *interconnectedness* among living creatures. In Chapter One we glanced at how scientists, with the aid of high-speed computers, have been able to penetrate a reality that is changing the way we perceive our world. As John Briggs* and F. David Peat* point out, "...randomness is interleaved with order, ...simplicity enfolds complexity, complexity harbors simplicity...." The "emerging science of wholeness" explores how everything in the cosmos is interconnected. In the healing arts, this discovery has come to the fore as well. Dolores Krieger, Ph.D., R.N., is the creative force behind *Therapeutic Touch*™ and put it plainly in a recent conversation: *"You don't stop at your skin!"* A broader, bolder vision of life is emerging, one which includes our dual citizenship in both physical and energetic realms. Within this model, our *interconnectedness* in a vast sea of life cannot be denied.

"We cannot live only for
ourselves.
A thousand fibers
connect us with
our fellow men; and
among those fibers,
as sympathetic threads,
our actions
run as causes, and they
come back to
us as effects."

Herman Melville

See "Suggested Reading" Appendix C

The following drama, which takes place just outside a fourth grade classroom in the Deep South, illustrates the interconnectedness of living things. It involves a science experiment inspired by the research of Marcel Vogel.* Vogel was the brilliant, award-winning IBM research scientist whose findings in the field of liquid crystals (whereby he concluded that *intent* manifests some type of energy field) inspired him to examine the effects of human thought and emotion on plants. Vogel affixed electrodes to his pet philodendron, then hooked it up to a galvanometer (lie-detector). The scientist would breathe deeply, relax, stand close to his philodendron and then let flow showers of affectionate intentions upon the plant as he held his hands, outstretched, towards it. As if on cue, the plant would respond with a series of ascending oscillations and corresponding leaf movements which, in repeated tests, would register on the galvanometer's recording chart! So, now our story begins.

The Power of Abundant Good Wishes: A True Story

*N*ot long ago, a curious fourth grade class read about Marcel Vogel's work in their *Weekly Reader*. They were intrigued with the notion of interconnectedness. A highly charged group of nine and ten year olds, they put their heads together to see if they could find their own clues about "the web of life." Deciding to prove to themselves the merits of this theory, each adopted a plant. Along the length of their portable classroom (a lightly constructed architectural afterthought more conducive to "open education" than its drab appearance implied), they dug a narrow plot. About mid-February, after lovingly and painstakingly planting a variety of botanical treasures, they began to observe and to "relate to" their plants, affectionately.

Across the way in another portable, the fifth grade teacher seemed to be forever feeding live rodents to that class's boa constrictor, but, the fourth-graders said they were more interested in experimenting in "creative," as opposed to "consumer" research and laughed about this. They wanted to "communicate" with their plants not only on a physical level but also on an "energy" level. Some of the sixth-graders, already firmly inured in the restrictive confines of a purely dualistic worldview, joked about this, but the fourth-graders, having the benefit of documented research, were sophisticated! They brushed aside disbelief and scoffing with the wise words, "Just wait and see!"

See "Suggested Reading" Appendix C

By May, all the plants were thriving, but those of two very "tuned-in" students were spectacular. Pedro, admired for his "good-eye" (focused eye) in baseball and a green thumb he attributed to working the fields before and after school, and poetic Beth, of the tender blue eyes, and quiet, gentle ways, who looked at her plant the way a new mother regards her baby, grew plants that were measurably larger than the others, and moved as the children stroked them from a good distance.

Everyone noticed!

By early June, a ritual of "live observation" of this artscience had evolved. The whole class would line up on the inside of the portable to peer out the generous windows. Beth and Pedro, on the outside and in full view of the fifth and sixth-graders, began their demonstration. They would smile at their plants as if they were their favorite schoolyard buddies, admire them and touch them gently. Next, stepping back a few inches they would begin to move their hands, repeatedly, from the top to the bottom of the plant, down-down-and-down again; until the leaves actually began to wave! A whole group of nine, ten, and eleven year old kids, not to mention a couple of amazed teachers, knew that they had encountered a force unseen.

Vogel, who in his Palo Alto lab had concluded that an invisible life-force envelopes living creatures, making possible "a mutual sensitivity allowing [us] not only to intercommunicate, but to record the communications," had nothing on these fourth-graders. They understood how the very real power of abundant good wishes expresses itself and affects other living creatures in an interconnected Whole. The students taught themselves and their community a good lesson in the realm of energetics, a good lesson in becoming aware of the dynamic interaction between the physical and energetic realms, a good lesson spotlighting the interconnectedness of all living creatures.

Try This Process: *Ki* Key I a

Interconnectedness acknowledged in empathic exchanges makes possible a dynamic interaction—in a multidimensional arena—where receptivity, reciprocity, and possibility blend in a cohesive way, towards balance. Here is an experiment in this energetic/physical phenomenon, which demonstrates the power of abundant good wishes. Try it.

The Power of Abundant Good Wishes: Experiment A, for *Beginners*, but not Just for Kids.	
• *Go to the garden shop or greenhouse of your choice. Select a packet of fast-growing seeds, and some excellent potting soil, and TWO smallish clay pots.*	
• *Next, from your favorite outdoor area, carefully retrieve a number of pebbles. Cleanse and place these in the base of each of the clay pots.*	
• *Now hand place the potting soil in both pots.* *Very important: At this point, select ONE container to which to pay special attention.*	
• *Now, LICK the inside of your LEFT palm, and put 5 seeds in it. Close your hand securely and cover it with your right hand. Hold the seeds in your hand for at least 3 minutes while intending abudant good wishes for those wee life forms. (Note if your hands heat up or tingle.)*	
• *Now plant the seeds as per package directions. Place them on your kitchen window sill. You will return 3 or more times each day to observe their progress, water them with non-chlorinated water, and lavish upon them your abundant good wishes.*	
• *In the other pot, plant 5 seeds in a casual way. Put this pot on a different window sill, and water it from time to time.*	
• *Keep a journal of your observations of the progress of the seeds in Pot #1 and Pot #2. At the end of one month, two months, three months, note differences between pots.*	
• *What does this experiment tell you about the Ki Keys of empathic resonance and interconnectedness?*	

Try This Process: *Ki* Key I b

Various energetic relationships exist in the interconnected multidimensional realm, where empathic exchanges have impact upon a whole system. Here is another experiment in energetics for you to try.

The Power of Abundant Good Wishes: Experiment B for *Intermediate* Students of All Ages	
• *Go to the garden shop or greenhouse of your choice. With the story of the fourth-graders in mind, try to tune-in to a section of plants with which you have an affinity.*	
• *Ask "permission" from one particular plant in this section to join you in an experiment.*	
• *Try to sense "consent," then bring this plant home.*	
• *Select a special place of honor for your particular plant. (You will be showering this small life-form with attention and nurturance for many months, so place it where you will remember to do this.)*	
• *Follow the procedure in the story of Abundant Good Wishes on the preceding pages.*	
• *Record notes and observations about your feelings and connections with this plant: physical feelings, emotional feelings, relationship feelings, energetic feelings.*	
What does this experiment tell you about empathic resonance and interconnectedness?	

Hint: philodendrons and geraniums are <u>very</u> receptive to interaction with human beings.

8

Openness and the Ki Channel

"The irresistible Vortex ... spins into itself always in the same direction...the whole Stuff of Things, from the most simple to the most complex; spinning into ever more comprehensive and astronomically complicated nuclei...and the result of this structural portion is an increase in consciousness.'

Pierre Teilhard de Chardin

Allowing

Presence
Spread your light
Through what is essentially empty.
Become transparent
In our midst
As we, in turn,
Become your conduits.

- Else -

What would the meadowlark
Do in the Spring
Could he not sing of
His fullest vocation —
To be the Window of the Creator —
To be the creation?

- And -

What would the artist
Do in her loft,
If not, soft
In transparent imagery,
Become herself,
Harmonious Consciousness?

Wind-in-the-Feather

II. Openness and the Ki Channel

*W*hat unknown worlds lie beyond those we perceive? In a realm where the customary (mechanistic/dualistic) view gives way to vast, untested possibility—where our senses are cleansed and renewed, where old patterns, self-images, and conditions loosen, and where opening to love, compassion and joy fosters equanimity, what new relationships may arise —in a *super-sensing world*. And how do we get there? Experiential forms of therapy such as Reiki have the capacity to dissolve barriers and resistances to "uncommon reaches," allowing us to migrate, through energetic portals, then to mediate the connection with multidimensional domains of existence. Reiki in particular offers an effective alternative to unfulfilling impulses by providing a structure within which individuals can make positive and lasting multidimensional changes in their lives.

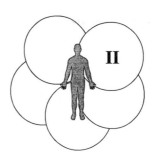

The first two elements of our earlier discussion, empathic resonance and awareness of our interconnectedness in a whole system, are in themselves potent nonphysical connections acting synergystically to power change. When they are combined with genuine openness and an awareness of vital Life-force, an exponentially significant shift can occur. These "distinguished energies" are interrelated, yet are as distinct as sound waves and heat waves, candlelight and firelight. How can we educate our senses towards such energetic transactions? Let's start with a close look at the following chart.

"Dwell as near as possible
to the channel
in which your life flows."

Henry David Thoreau

Journal

Try This Process: *Ki* Key II a
What You Already Know May Surprise You

If you have a total of three or more yes answers, you know about Ki, and if you, like most people, answered "yes" to some, or all, of these questions, you have already experienced Ki, and through it, your connection with a world of possibility.

Have you ever walked into a business meeting late, and, in the silence, "felt" the air charged with "electricity"?
☐ Yes   ☐ No

Have you ever "felt" someone walking behind you, even though you could not see the person, or "felt" drained or exhilarated around another?   ☐ Yes   ☐ No

Have you ever squinted at the area surrounding the plants in a summer garden, just after it rains, and "imagined" you saw a mirage-like, transparent energy there?
☐ Yes   ☐ No

Has your whole body gotten "jumpy" during a thunderstorm?
☐ Yes   ☐ No

Has someone you were to meet walked into a crowded room and headed straight toward you, even though s/he'd never met you or had any idea of who you were?
☐ Yes   ☐ No

Can you tell how someone's feeling just by the "atmosphere" around them, even though they may tell you that they are feeling differently than what you think?
☐ Yes   ☐ No

Have you ever been daydreaming about your favorite person in the world, and suddenly felt a surge in energy?
☐ Yes   ☐ No

Has your hair ever "stood on end" when someone walked by you? Have you ever liked or disliked someone on first sight?
☐ Yes   ☐ No

Ki Works with Openness

*T*he previous *process* exercise may have surprised you with what you already have experienced in the way of life-force energy, but the scientific community has been investigating this field for some time, and is quite familiar with such things. There is increasing scientific evidence that living things emit detectable electromagnetic fields, just as the Earth itself and every component on it radiates energy. We know that the human body, even though it may appear solid, is far from it—and that it contains electrically charged particles and has an electrical output of its own—(this, measurable by sensitive superconducting machines). Moreover, Dr. William A. Tiller*, Professor Emeritus of Stanford University and pioneering researcher of subtle energy, who began his work in the 1970's demonstrated the existence of an energy field *not* in the electromagnetic spectrum, which responds to *intentional human focus*.

But such amazing topics have been explored for thousands of years. Harmony and disharmony, balance and imbalance (energy polarity or the yin and yang of the Chinese model) are not new concepts. For millennia, most eastern cultures considered the balancing of "flowing energies" to be responsible for the regulation of mind-body systems and processes. Hence, neither space nor time could restrain vital energy exchange (only a lack of focused concentration). Adepts of spiritual traditions, known for their ability to focus and for reaching states of expanded awareness, knew the art of connecting with a universal stream of vital energy, the basic source of life called *Prana* (in the tradition of India), *Ch'i* (in China) and *Ki* (Japan). Eastern adepts from as far back as 5000 B.C. were joined in their recognition of Life-force energy by western scientific thinkers in about 500 B.C., when Pythagoras noted its

"The soul should always stand ajar, ready to welcome the ecstatic experience."

Emily Dickinson

See Suggested Reading, Appendix C, Energy Medicine.

effects. Current research in "subtle energy" demonstrates that living creatures exist *in resonance with* different energy frequencies. Now mythological images come into new focus as their description of the body human's energy centers (*chakras*), said to be cone-shaped energy vortices within which spiraling action takes place, are plotted with ultra-sensitive equipment in scientific labs, and *Ki is defined as that alive energy that permeates all living things.*

Awareness of *Ki* can be vague at first, but increases when we begin to recognize it in everyday encounters, such as those in the previous checklist. Then we discover that we are alive with *Ki*. It is always present and available. Plants have it. Kids in the school yard have it. "Couch potatoes" have it. Lovers snuggling have it. Poets and programmers have it. You have it. I have it. All living creatures *have* it. The question is not if we have it, but is *how do we become consciously and consistently aware of Ki.* One method may be to engage this energetic phenomenon through practicing contemplation. Reiki facilitates the process because recognizing *Ki* is a natural result of the increased awareness of vital Life-force garnered in the practice of Reiki. The more you allow yourself to sink into the stillness of the Reiki moment, and the more sensitive you become to your own energy vacillations and to those of others, the easier it becomes to recognize *Ki*. We will explore this later on in the book. In the meantime, try the *processes* at the end of this chapter.

Some people see *Ki* in halos and auras, but most people do not. That is not because they cannot, or because it does not exist or even because they don't "believe." It is just because they are untrained. Training yourself to recognize *Ki* can be fun and interesting. If you do not trust what you cannot see, you might try something more technologically sophisticated than your own crude physical instruments (eyes, ears, etc.). We mentioned that in the late 1970s Dr. William A. Tiller* put together a team of researchers who were equipped with such ultra-sensitive measuring devices which they developed. Tiller and his colleagues pioneered laboratory studies evidencing the existence of multidimensional levels of the extended energetic framework of human beings. They dubbed this the human energy field (HEF).

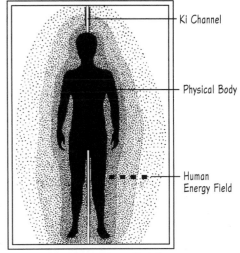

Human Energy Field (HEF)

Operating on the assumption that there could be "higher dimensional phenomena" and extrapolating on the Einstein model which relates energy to matter ($E=mc^2$), Tiller asserted that a storehouse of potential energy exists within the tiniest particle of matter, and focused on exploring the possibility suggested in the (later) Einstein-Lorentz Transformation Equation (which provided new insights into the dimensional aspects of matter) and into the exponential relationship between matter and energy. Tiller was questioning the assumption that matter cannot be accelerated beyond the speed of light. He was fascinated with how subtle energetic interactions of living systems worked, and interested in practical applications for this research in "positive space time." What would be the properties of particles traveling at supraluminal velocities? *Could human consciousness influence a subtle energetic body? Could certain thoughts exist as "thought forms" in the energetic fields of the thinker?*

---

*See Suggested Reading, Appendix C, Energy Medicine.

(These questions would later be considered by Rupert Sheldrake in his research suggesting that "morphogenic fields are responsible for the characteristic form and organization of systems at all levels of complexity... [and have] characteristic structures." (Rupert Sheldrake, *A New Science of Life*, p. 13.)

As research progressed, Tiller postulated that a physical-etheric interface exists, allowing a continuous stream of *Universal Life-force Energy* to catalyze in and to interact in multidimensional transactions at physical/energetic and higher levels. This available flow, known as *Ki, Ch'i, Qi,* and *Prana,* Tiller demonstrated to be a beneficial, vital resonant energy which *extends beyond the surface of living things.* In the human being, it brightens the area around the body—(you do have an aura), especially the head (you do have a halo!). What Tiller and his associates began as research in the *Human Energy Field* (HEF) has become a promising field of scientific investigation with potential for wellness in the years to come, in such areas as: coronary artery disease, psychoneuro-immunology, laser surgery, hormonal therapy, nutrition, and stress-related disease. One of the most interesting applications of subtle energy research in which Tiller himself is today a directing force is underway at the Institute of HeartMath* in Boulder Creek, California, where Rollin McCraty, Mike Atkinson and Glen Rein, explorers in new science technologies, have suggested a new discipline: cardioneuroimmunology (CNI).

See Appendix C, Energy Medicine.

In a paper published in the proceedings of the annual Conference of The International Society for the Study of Subtle Energies and Energy Medicine*(ISSSEE), researchers concluded that:

"There is a correlation between the subjects' mental and emotional states and the frequency spectra of the ECG. When the subjects sincerely felt love, care, or appreciation, the spectra changed to a more ordered and coherent frequency distribution. On the other hand, when the subjects were in a state of frustration, worry, or anger, the ECG spectra was disordered and chaotic. Heart frequencies create an electromagnetic field which is distributed throughout the body. The degree of coherence in the heart is the major determining factor for coherence in the rest of the body, suggesting the possibility that ECG frequencies have profound effects on overall health and well being. Psychological evaluations confirmed that subjects who produced higher percentages of coherent ECG frequencies were better able to manage their mental and emotional natures and their reactions to stressful events in day-to-day life."

When these studies are considered in conjunction with a study by Randolph C. Byrd, MD, of the positive therapeutic effects of intercessory prayer in a coronary care unit population, we may begin to appreciate the extent to which subtle human energy fields operate within a whole system. And the practice of Reiki moves in this arena.

In the practice of Reiki, we are *consciously* tapping into *Universal Life-force Energy* to experience the powerful effects of the integrating action, which accelerates healing. Being in this *process* involves learning to cut through illusion. Then we can come to realize that we are not just physical beings in a physical reality. We are also vibrant, vibrating energy systems! The practice of Reiki can help us to relax into feeling comfortable as we assimilate this information, which hundreds of years and hundreds of scientists, in conscientious enterprise, have produced.

"With Reiki,
there is always hope."

Hawayo Takata

See Appendix C, Energy Medicine.

To *experience* multidimensional perception in a fabric of *being* that is close to, as well as *beyond*, our bodies is a possibility for all Reiki practitioners! Reiki is a simple methodology for accessing life-force energy which is available, open to, surging through/with*in* and with*out* all living creatures, in the spaces between us, that indeed *unite* us! We, as vibrating fields of multidimensional energy, are *in* the cosmos, as the cosmos is *in* us. After millions of years of evolutionary unfolding, we are opening to *a new way of seeing* our own nature.

New Images

Contemporary research confirms what mystics have always believed. There exists a subtle energy field encompassing living creatures in a whole, vibrant, resonating system. In the human being, these fields are known as "subtle bodies." Once described in ancient texts, they can now be detected by scientific instruments as they "vibrate" beyond our physical extremities. This is not mysticism, or wishful thinking. This is real. Scientists worldwide have demonstrated that we can perceive energy extending beyond all living creatures, that we can delineate the subtle bodies just beyond our physical ones and that we can become familiar with these energy bodies and their patterns of moving energy. Adjusting to this new worldview can be challenging for a populace raised on baseball, apple pie, a solid work ethic, and the good old dependable dualistic model of reality. Still, every day scientific research is corroborated. My own personal experience over the past ten years and that of hundreds of my colleagues testifies to this.

Many "normal, reasonable" folks, such as Norm, have moved off the comfortable ladder of the "apparent," and stepped beyond to the new and heightened awareness of this emerging understanding—much as once we moved beyond the notion that the world is flat. Some otherwise "ordinary" people have learned to recognize certain energy patterns as having particular significance, as Norm did in his statement, "What makes a place special is the *energy*." Others recognize that there are energy patterns relative to growth, healing, and general well-being.

One such person, a medical doctor who "reads" auras, is Robert T. Jaffe, M.D., a private practioner in Arizona. As a medical doctor, Dr. Jaffe operates within specified legal constraints. He must substantiate diagnoses he makes as a result of his perceptions of the subtle bodies. Indeed, he insists upon documentation of his observations with laboratory analysis. Results confirm his diagnoses. Over the years the word about this has gotten around, and now Dr. Jaffe not only practices allopathic and wholistic medicine, but also teaches doctors, nurses, and others interested in subtle energy *how* to perceive it. He maintains that such vision is not difficult to achieve once one is attuned to it. He also maintains that a problem which resides in the "mind-body," can influence one's whole being, causing "a twisting, or contraction of the energy field."

As scientific researchers develop new imaging technologies such as the Magnetic Resonance Imager (MRI) CT Scanner and PEI Scanner, physicians and other therapists will have tools with which to explore the uses of *Ki* for balancing a multidimensional body. In the meantime, before "twisted energy" moves into your body, you can release it energetically through a combination of Reiki, contemplative relaxation, an understanding of what the root causal factors are, and knowledge of how energy flows.

"We are always and everywhere connected to the Source."

Robert Jaffe, M.D.
In a lecture at Whole Life Expo

Expanding on that thought for a moment, we see how it is possible that *we are participants with, rather than controllers of the process of Wellness or Wholeness—a significant benchmark in our unfolding process.*

"Wonder, miracle emcompasses...man; he lives in an element of miracle...."

Thomas Carlyle
Portraits of John Knox

Human beings are dynamic energy systems interconnected in an organic way to all living creatures and to Earth Mother. As we know, the world is not static; it is dynamic. If we replace reductionist, purely physical reality thinking, applying synthesis/systems thinking, we can develop new relationships within ourselves and among living communities. Through earnest enterprise, we can dissolve unhealthy restrictive energy patterns. We can see our way to a new commitment, and with it a new hope, for ourselves and for the global community.

This means that, by arranging pictures in my mind of Wholeness (Wellness) in the world-at-large, by telling "my" story that touches everyone, all creatures around me, in an integral, natural community reflective of the fully functioning me, I participate as a catalyst for change in the *new* story. This is the larger meaning of energy flow in the big picture.

Before developing new inner/outer vision, however, we need to have an *awareness,* we need to "see" energy. Today's technology can and does aid us. In fact, scientists have established "maps" of the pathways of flowing energy and documented this in their laboratories. They have demonstrated that energy flow has direction, and that the flow is visible and registers (even sometimes to the human eye).

So, what is seen?

Energy Patterns, Pathways and Message Centers

£nergy patterns and pathways are observable: *Ki,* (life-force energy), moves from the head downward, through trunk, arms, hands, legs and feet, along meridians in the body, through a series of "chakras," energy centers. It concentrates around living things, as a field of energy; in human beings, the HEF. It also extends out in space as an overall life-force field, as evidenced in scientific laboratories, with ultra-sensitive Geiger counter-type measuring devices, as evidenced in research documenting the healthful benefits of meditation and intercessory prayer,* thus confirming the belief melodies of philosophers, mystics, and healers regarding the existence of chakras in the body. The implications of this fact are far-reaching.

The stunning revelation that *living creatures are interconnected in a resonating field of energy* demands considerable rethinking and reorientation of attitude and belief. Although Eastern thought for millennia has claimed the existence of energy centers in the human body, only recently has that perennial wisdom come to light in the Western mind. Scientists have discovered seven major "message centers" and at least six lesser ones along energy pathways in the body human, and in so doing have confirmed an intuitive perceptual understanding thousands of years old. Chakras observed in the past can now, through sensitive instruments, can be observed as highly resonant spinning vortices of energy. The word *chakra* itself, which comes from the Sanskrit word for wheel, depicts the swirling action of this energy center.

"None of these visions ever quite deluded him. At any moment, by an effort of his will, he could discern substances through their misty lack of substance...."

Nathaniel Hawthorne
The Scarlet Letter

See Suggested Reading, Appendix C, Energy Medicine Research, Articles and Abstracts.

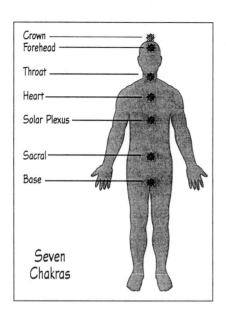

Crown
Forehead
Throat
Heart
Solar Plexus
Sacral
Base

Seven
Chakras

Chakras could be likened to super computers, processing data which is coming in and out, and "crunching" it in a dynamic fashion, before distributing the information. However, in the case of *chakras,* the exchange is energetic. Each of the chakras is said to resonate with a certain sound, color, and frequency, and can be stimulated and balanced.

We can gain access to the chakras and activate innate healing capacities in a variety of ways. I think the most readily available way is through the practice of Reiki. As a matter of fact, Reiki I Training *focuses* on the endocrine system which correlates directly with the seven major Chakras. *(See Chart.)*

Ki flows in, out, about, and through living creatures, freely, and in a balanced way, when you are feeling relaxed and well. However, if you are feeling distressed or very ill, the flow of *Ki* is blocked, scattered, or diminished as evidenced in current medical research in stress and mind-body interactions.

Knowing about these exchanges and recognizing *Ki* can be a gentle prelude to learning how to *open to, or to attune to its restorative effects.* Only then is it possible to intersect with or "draw" *Ki.* One of my teachers advised me to think of this action as committing to good banking practices. "Fiscal exchanges of an energy sort," she admonished, "but first, you must *open* the account and utilize this agent of change!"

Openness: The Conduit for *Ki* and for Drawing *Ki* from the "Bank of Universal Life-force."

*L*ike empathic resonance, openness is an energetic key which works in tandem with Life-force energy to create change. Then, one opens one's heart—not for self, or for an immediate situation—but instead, for a deeper understanding of the *universal experience,* where one clears a space for relaxing into harmony with the Whole. Openness means being available to view the wider picture without being locked into responses or patterns of behavior. If someone criticizes you, for example, whereas you might have retaliated in kind with criticism (on one end of the continuum) or simply shut down on the other end, now you are staying with the moment, staying present, open to the *exact experience* of what you are *feeling,* right there and then. You are saying to yourself, "WHAT am I feeling?" This has the effect of keeping you *in* the moment and of expanding perception. Here, you are not seeking self-improvement, but rather the potential to learn something new without falling into a dualistic conversation (good vs. bad) with yourself or anyone else. You are putting a personal agenda aside, putting aside judgement, blaming, acting out, or repressing in order to create a space for *possibility.*

"Joy is the sweet voice,
joy the luminous cloud.
We in ourselves rejoice!
And thence flows all that
charms or ear or sight,
All melodies the echoes
of that voice,
All colours a suffusion
from the light."

Samuel Taylor Coleridge

You are learning to relax. When you are relaxing, you are also more easily able to access a field of resonating vital energy. When your mind remains unbiased, neutral, and not grasping in judgment, when your heart beats with unconditional love and caring (when you are able to open your heart and open your mind), dimensions then appear as you come to an awareness of the field of pure possibility.

Try This Process: *Ki* Key II b
Recognizing the Open Channel

Follow the directions below to discover a first-hand experience of recognizing the "empty" channel of pure potential and note this.

Journal

Recognizing the Channel	
• After reading the section on the energetic *Ki* key of Openness, put down the book to investigate further.	
• Draw an aromatic, relaxing bath.	
• Light a candle.	
• Get in.	
• Relax, but stay alert.	
• After you have enjoyed the bath, open the drain all the way, and closely observe the swirling vortex at that drain (a whirlpool in your bathtub).	
• Note that at the center, within this spiraling flow of water, just as within the "eye" of a hurricane, there is an **empty channel**.	
• Recognize this **emptiness** as **possibility**.	
• Make a mental note to let this bathtub vortex represent the **open channel**, the conduit accessed in the practice of Reiki, which connects us with a resonating whole system.	

Open the Account

*W*hen *openness* combines with other energetic keys in the practice of Reiki, a quality of holding a "space" for something occurs, as we have just seen in the process *"Ki Key II b."* We could compare this action, as well, to holding a "space" in a bank, by opening a bank account, a space in which one may deposit, withdraw, or transact exchanges and funnel them. *Openness* is an energetic key; when practiced in Reiki, it has that quality of holding a space. It then can be seen as *opportunity*. With the slightest mental adjustment, just a bit of imagery, it is possible to "open the account" and utilize this agent of change.

> "Remember, all situations are passing memory."
>
> Chinese Proverb

The empty channel you observed in your bathtub is a metaphor for the *openness* described by many practitioners of Reiki. Openness allows for the transference of *Ki*. This is a life-affirming transaction, which manifests the opportunity to find wellness on multidimensional levels, inner vision and inner wisdom, and supports a give-and-take, making one available both to share *Ki* and to draw upon *Ki*. Openness, as *experienced* in the practice of Reiki, creates a possibility for abundance, change, nurturance, and accelerates healing on a personal and global level.

> "When one learns letting go and letting be, when one learns sinking, when one learns emptying and being emptied, one necessarily comes face to face with nothingness...."
>
> Matthew Fox

After you have seen a whirlpool (or vortex) and the open channel within it in the "comfort of your own home" so to speak, it is easy to imagine, is it not? What you might not have known is that the *process* is also quite simple, and simply delightful. Is visualizing *Ki* being *drawn* through the open place within that swirling mass of energy something you can experience?

It is easy to draw energy from the *"Bank of Ki"* in the Reiki *experience*. The act of deciding to *draw* it, "conscious intention," creates the possibility, or *openness*. This is the "secret" necessary for the transmission of vital energy. In other words, when you decide to take good care of youself, as a unique, connected member of our living cosmos, you carve a space within yourself that is ready to accept abundant blessings. You are in a *process of being* in which all *beingness* is available for you and through you to an organic whole system. When we come to a comprehensive awareness of the interdependence (and interconnectedness) of all life on our planet, when we come to see Mother Earth as what she is —a living, organic, unfolding phenomenon—and when we see ourselves not just as observers, but as participants in a dynamic evolutionary unfolding, then the *"Bank of Ki"* holds the promise of beneficial development and reenergizing transactions.

"One of the most pernicious illusions developed in the heart of man during the course of history is the pseudo-evidence of his completeness and fixity."

Pierre Teilhard de Chardin

In this endeavor, you are not trying to get certain results. You are simply making yourself available (OPEN) to "being" energized. You are, therefore, consciously allowing. Reiki is a *being* artscience in which you can reach a special state, (called passive volition) that says: "Never mind hanging on to your personal (ego) defense. Never mind results! Just **BE, Now!**" In this enterprise called "just being and relaxing," listen to what your inner voice is saying. What do you feel as you recognize the nonlocal, nonphysical quality of *openness*? What are your impressions as you hold an understanding of the important key to profound relaxation, and a bold view of yourself as a *physical and energetic citizen of the Universe?* *

<hr>

**See Appendix E., Energy Medicine Research, Articles and Abstracts.*

Try This Process: *Ki* Key II c
Tuning-In

Follow the directions below to discover a first-hand experience of recognizing multidimensional energy and note this.

Tuning-In to the Energetic Sphere	
• *Sit quietly in your office or personal space at home, or in a place in the natural world.*	
• *Breathe deeply, feel your muscles begin to relax.*	
• *Cover your eyes with your hands. (Keep your thumbs in.)*	
• *Ask a friend to move into the area as silently as a black cat at midnight.*	
• *Pay attention. Can you "feel" or "sense" when your friend is present?*	
• *Try this often until you **notice**.*	
• *If you are tuning-in, on many levels, to someone else's energetic sphere, you are tuning-in on many levels, to Ki!*	
• *Detail your observations.*	

Journal

**Try This Process: *Ki* Key II d
Drawing *Ki* From the Bank**

Follow the directions below to discover energetic transactions, and note this.

Journal	Drawing Energy from the Whole System	
	• *Use your imagination. Visualize a vortex. Pretend you are a whirlpool of human energy, with a highly charged "channel" which starts near your "halo" above the top of your head.*	
	• *Get a clear image of this in your mind's eye—you, as a human "whirlpool." Get comfortable with this image, possibly draw it on a photo of yourself until it is very clear.*	
	• *Now visualize Ki, like life-glitter swishing into your channel from the energetic spaces just beyond your body.*	
	• *Visualize yourself drinking in (drawing) revitalizing energy through the crown of your head, and throughout every system of your body. If you can imagine it, try this with the multidimensional, subtle body.*	
	• *Next, imagine sharing this energy in a living, whole system with others, and with the global community.*	

Try This Process: *Ki* Key II e
Relaxing, Opening, Celebrating

Use the following step-by-step formula to discover energy medicine.
Note before and after sensations.

Connecting with Possibility	
• Sit quietly.	
• Breathe deeply. (See Breathing technique, Appendix B.) Inhale. Release with compassion all that is heavy and distressing in your life. Exhale.	
• Center yourself in an open nonlocal space; and continue conscious breathing.	
• Note that you are consciously breathing in difficulties, releasing them to breathe out freshness for all living creatures.	
• Fold your hands over your heart, thumbs in.	
• Now, envision a peaceful, safe place in which you are secure and can rest.	
• Pretend you are a living vessel, a fantabulous, enormous redwood tree just waiting to drink in the elixir of life, and connect with the open channel of pure potential.	
• Keep breathing, consciously. Keep hands folded over heart, thumbs in.	
• Focus your attention by holding the image you have created of a tranquil place, and the open awaiting receptacle.	
• Relax, and Open to possibility; feel Ki flowing, naturally, being drawn like the warmth of sunlight to every part of you —easing tension, replenishing deficits, melting away obstructions—leaving you relaxed, renewed, refreshed— able to share new vigor with the human community and with the world-at-large. Celebrate the welcomed sense of connectedness with the ground of all being.	

Journal

9

"Alpha" and Alpha!

"Too swift arrives as tardy as too slow."

William Shakespeare

A Code

Viewing Life

Lie on your back
'neath the trees in the Spring.
Let your nose be your guide
whilst faeries Sing.

Slide your eyes down the tip
to the leaves at the Top.

Daydream, on the ground,
of Life without stop!

See, in the sky,
a stream passing by.

Join it there, with your Heart;
In Mid-air....

Wind-in-the-Feather

III. "Alpha" and Alpha!, Twin Ki Keys

*D*id you know that we can train our brains to produce the electrical output most conducive to "passive volition?" The training is called "alpha biofeedback," from the brain wave pattern induced, and from the method of induction. Since the *Alpha* state is particularly conducive to suspending tension and appears to offer an alternative to years of practice in various forms of meditation (which also produces the desired state) it has become quite popular. How did this come about, and how does it relate to *Ki-Key III*?

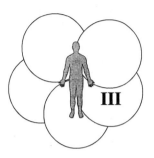

In the early 1940s, when biofeedback was in its infancy, researchers discovered that the brain wave activity of their subjects fell in step with the same pattern of light emission as was seen in flickering firelight. They were able to measure the electrical output of the brain in the resulting relaxed but alert state. It was characterized by an EEG pattern showing bursts of alpha (8 to 13hz) and frequencies ranging in amplitude from 150uv or more—*the same as those measured in meditators.* Other researchers found that subjects exhibiting increased coherence of brain wave activity and hemispheric synchronization displayed properties beyond those we experience in waking consciousness—properties of highly focused awareness, where subjects were able to tap into latent capacities— even to gain access to hierarchial levels of information enfolded within the structure of matter/energy fields and space itself.

Yogis meditating in exotic temples and scouts telling tales by campfire have much in common. Research proves this. Findings indicate that these two very diverse groups, in approaching a relaxed, but alert state, both produce higher levels of serotonin and beta endorphin neuro-chemicals, and experience significant muscular relaxation.* Another interesting research discovery is that once *you* are aware of the "Alpha state," you can reproduce it at will! Like riding a bike, once you know how, *you know how*! Researchers are now documenting how achieving this state is readily available through the practice of Reiki.

Somewhere between biofeedback, scouting, and years of consistent meditation in a nonlocal space requiring only your committed willingness and attention, lies the practice of Reiki. Here, many Reiki participants and most experienced practioners produce Alpha automatically and easily identify and use it.

If there is a "how to" in the practice of Reiki, it is "how to" reach this state. That is why we have included practical *process experiments* on the following pages. Here you may determine your personal ability to notice and access multidimensional energetic tools. Just *being* or just *doing nothing at all,* in the Reiki Session may lead to the alert but relaxed state of Alpha, which is a by-product of the Reiki process. No effort required! It just *happens*, as part of the artscience.

The following processes can be helpful in practicing recognition of Alpha, and they can also be fun to experience!

See Appendix C., Energy Medicine Research, Articles and Abstracts.

Try This Process: *Ki* Key III a
The "Alpha" Nature Walk

Here is a 21-Day Process which you may use in conjunction with The 21-Day Reiki and Relaxation program. It requires your relaxed, alert attention in a natural setting and your written processing of the experiences.

Journal

• *To recognize "Alpha," Alpha! take an "Alpha Walk" in the natural world even just for ten or fifteen minutes, twice a day, for three weeks (21 days).*

• *Pay close attention to what attracts you as you connect with your surroundings. Note this.*
Is it a certain tree? A soft chirp? An open meadow?

• *Ask permission of this natural source of interest to sit quietly and to observe; wait to feel consent. You will sense whether there is consent or not. Note this:*

• *As you sit quietly, cover your eyes with your hands (thumbs in) and try to "breathe" with the energy channel (as discussed in Ki Key II) which connects you with the whole natural system.*

• *Now, open your eyes.*

• *Observe closely.*

• *Make mental notes. You will be journaling later.*

• *Notice how tuned in, relaxed but aware you are.*

• *Later, journal your experience in detail.*

• *At the end of 21 days, compile your notes into story form, one that could be told by campfire.*

This is an adaptation of an exercise from a pioneer in the field of Ecopsychology, Dr. Michael Cohen, whose book *Reconnecting with Nature* is a favorite of ours.

Journal

Try This Process: *Ki* Key IIIb
Just Be, Right Here and Now!

Recognizing and being able to move to "Alpha" and Alpha!
is important. If you are a keen, competent, and confident
obeserver of NOW, you will surely recognize "Alpha" and Alpha!

• Stay present.
• Take a relaxing, deep, deep breath...and just let go....
• In and out—breathing, now—notice your breathing.
• Now, pretend you are playing baseball and it is your turn up to bat, and you have got your eye on the ball ("good eye").
• Stay with the sense of the moment for so long as you can—and keep breathing.
• Balance yourself between being relaxed and being alert, and keep focused for a minute, or two, or five, or—here's Alpha!
• Journal your observations.

Try This Process: *KI* Key IIIc
Concentrated Focus

Now find activities in which you can actually experience periods of relaxed but focused processing. Engage in these activities at least three times a week. Use this page for noting your experiences.

Journal

10

Integrity and Core Harmony

"I am for those tiny, invisible, loving human forces that work from individual to individual, creeping through the crannies of the world like so many rootlets... which, if given time, will rend the hardest monuments of human pride."

William James

Centered

At the Crossroads of Spacetime,
of Here and Now,
At that Moment,
Lies Potentiality...

And a Choice of
Whether to be alert to the Moment,
Or to risk losing contact with Self
In veiled moments
Extending on, and on...

Into a Lifetime
Of Illusion.

Wind-in-the-Feather

IV. Integrity and Core Harmony

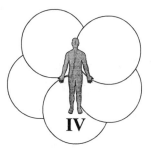

*A*s children, relatively few of us were loved unconditionally, and thus, in tender years, as we were separated from love, we learned *fear*. Then we learned to create and to hide behind imaginary faces which we created as coping mechanisms. Each of these "masks" expressed a bit of the *fear* that we were not lovable or capable; each mask became a character in a childhood drama of our own making, where we played the role of "victim" or "saint," "clod" or "perfectionist." We bought into an *illusion*, and with this *pain*, at very deep levels. But pain is also the great dissolver of illusion, if we choose to regard it as such, and in the same way, masks can be opportunities, if we learn to unveil the fresh faces beneath them. While each character we once created has left its mark on multidimensional aspects of self, and silently has become so familiar and comfortable that we began to believe ourselves to *be* the roles we played, each imaginary face is subject to change. Each character is the fabrication of a wounded child. Each mask disguises a cry for healing. Behind the bravado of the "bully" lies the brave heart of an adventurer. The "victim," healed, opens with empathy for others (as Princess Diana demonstrated in her humanitarian endeavors not long ago, while a grateful world watched). To dissolve the subpersonalities we create as children, we must become *conscious* of them. We must choose to bear the fruit of our inner being.

If the energetic dynamos of *Empathic Resonance* in combination with *Interconnectedness*, *Ki*, *Openness* and "*Alpha!*" deal directly with present moment *experience,* the next *Ki*-Keys, *Integrity and Core Harmony*, treat the subject of the inner tensions arising from spanning time, from past to future, as we, as physical beings in a multidimensional reality, observe that *choice* affects coherence, affects our well-being.

> "What's in a name? That which we call a rose by any other name would smell as sweet."
>
> William Shakespeare

To choose, in stillness at "the crossroads," means to become aware of the inner tensions arising from spanning time, from past to future. We become conscious, when we pause to *be* in the *Now*. Let me explain. Deep within us is an inner knowledge of the richness of the *new*, which yearns for recognition. By being mindful in the moment, the "Witness Self" participates in the *experience,* the *process,* which is anchored in the *new*, or the *Now*. We can perceive our internal space with clarity, find inner wisdom, as well as moderate our external space. We can facilitate accepting ourselves. We can draw upon the full extent of our *being*, but this is easier to do if we are *present in the moment*.

The practice of Reiki can release the tension of concealed injury, the pain of the past, the unprocessed experience, and can lessen insecurity borne of an unknown future which impacts our processes to the core. In her books and workshops, psychologist and Reiki Master Paula Horan, Ph.D. deals extensively with *Core Self.* She refers to *Core Self* as the very heart of your Being, the real, limitless You. "It is totally uplifting [to] experience your true identity and potential," she says, and goes on to point out that Reiki (the *experience* and *energy*) "will eventually guide you to the experience that you, yourself, *are* Reiki, or *Universal Life-force Energy*."

Being centered, in your business life or in your personal life, starts with self-inquiry, an inner vision of You, within and without, in relationship to the Whole. You have heard the advice, "To thine own self be true." Have you ever wondered just who *You* are, the "True *You?*" You may not explore these questions frequently, yet until you know *who you are* and then relax into accepting and being yourself, how can you relate to yourself or to others, freely and wholeheartedly?

I am reminded of the Tibetan chant, *Om mani padme hum*—Absolute One, creating, maintaining, and dissolving into bliss, is the jewel in the heart of the Lotus, and is none other than *my true self*—which, using the opening lotus blossom as a symbol, depicts the unity of the individual being with all that is, as it unfolds to wholeness.

When a person really relaxes into being just who that person is, the synergy of *Integrity and Core Harmony* in relationship to *potential* together with other energetic keys, combines to influence a trajectory towards wellness—on many levels. This trajectory begins during infancy and childhood, when the quality of tactuality experienced in eye contact, tender touch, emotional nurturance produces the appropriate changes in the brain, as well as healthy growth and development of end organs in the skin, writes Ashley Montagu* (in *Touching, The Human Significance of the Skin*, p. 265).

"Bodily connectedness is the basis of that interconnectedness with others that we call sociality and this is brought about by the closeness of mother and child in infancy. Such a close bodily relationship is the basis of good feelings about oneself, and the feeling of bodily connectedness leads to a feeling of self-esteem. Fundamentally the source of self-esteem is love."*

"There are no static objects called the Self and the World. Instead there is a web of shifting relationships in which, by a strange inversion of usual logic, the relationship comes before the things related."

C.J.S. Clarke
Reality through the Looking-Glass

---

*See Appendix C, Suggested Reading

If a lack of loving *touch* during preverbal and early childhood periods of development is experienced as separation anxiety, and generates such feelings as loneliness, frustration, isolation, experienced as a loss of unconditional love. Can the ancient practice, extending into remote antiquity, of "laying on of hands" foster a notable contrast in the resulting malaise, and thus positively influence and even heal these early wounds? Over the years, I have come to see that, through the practice of Reiki, the practice of *healing touch*, this can be so!

Through the practice of Reiki, it becomes apparent that being "in integrity" with yourself means releasing life strategies that are self-defeating, unfulfilling, or worse. The opportunity to self-actuate, or to live up to your own potential, becomes a much more appealing and satisfying prospect. A fundamental and compelling drive towards a field of *possibility* arises. Reiki practice structures the opportunity for you to recognize and to synchronize with "true Self." In the Reiki *experience,* you come in contact with your natural ability to cope with difficult situations, to resolve sticky issues or relationships, to release stress, to enjoy inner peace, to contribute to the community, and to contribute to global well-being—and that's just a short list! Indeed, Reiki practice and participation facilitates opening to and celebrating life, while you are just *being* where you are, when you are there—merely being present!

Try This Process: *Ki* Key IV
Connecting with Core Self
Follow the process below, journaling your responses.

* *Imagine, or go to, a summer meadow where scent, sound, color, attractive spaces, shafts of light, and mysterious possibility dwell.*

* *Now, imagine that you are gently swaying in a soft, woven hammock, resting in a beautiful space of pure potential.*

* *Relax, and focus your attention on your breathing. Bravely breathe in all distress.*

* *Notice the distress. Notice it as a phenomenon common to all living creatures, and compassionately release it.*

* *Now, slowly exhale, and with this breath out, send abundant blessings to all living creatures.*

* *Continue to watch your breath and your breathing until you are totally aware of it—breathing in distress, breathing out good wishes.*

* *Now place your hands on your knee and focus your attention on it. (This evokes a conscious experience of Now awareness in which your physical body grounds your attention). See how this experience combines both physicality and energetics and is aligned with your true nature.*

* *From this process you may connect with who you are—your Core Self—and get in touch with the integrity of that Being.*

Journal

11

Attending Now and Being

*"Supposing...we now try, if only by some trick of the mind,
to shift our outlook unreservedly into that of the World which is revolving?"*

Pierre Teilhard de Chardin

no barriers
no boundaries
no hierarchies
separate us
in the realm of pure potential

Wind-in-the-Feather

V. Attending Now and Being

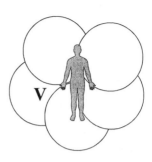

*T*he enterprise of discovering and honoring your Core Self requires *focus*. *Focus is the ability to pay attention, in a present moment, to **being** where you are.* If you intend, through your commitment, to manifest well-being (for example, to balance relaxation, stress, and anxiety) and so become more aware of multidimensional energetic transactions, you will need to be able to quiet persistent rumblings of your "logical" mind, to focus upon the *Here and Now.*

The Reiki methodology centers around the practice of *Attending Now and Being,* and can enable you to summon up a point of stillness through visualization and imagining. This practice asks: "Where can you go in your mind's eye to seek focus? If you see empty spaces as possibilities, where in your imagination do you feel grounded in groundlessness and centered in an ocean of pure potentiality?" Reiki practice promises that if you find "present moment staying power," all possibility opens to you, and opens the way for you to *be* this.

Mindfulness is about *being* in a state of wakefulness, with all its unique possibilities, about *being* awake to each moment as it unfolds. While it is natural for our minds to go on "automatic pilot," scattering seeds of thought here and there along the way, we can bring the mind back home through mindfulness training and practice. In so doing, we can focus different aspects of our multidimensional being while calming all the warring fragments of self, dissolving internal stress, supporting self-understanding, defusing negativity and aggression, and viewing turbulent emotions and thoughts with acceptance.

Sogyal Rinpoche says that this "…wise generosity has the flavor of boundless space, so warm and cozy that you feel enveloped and protected by it as if by a blanket of sunlight." (Quoted from Sogyal Rinpoche's *The Tibetan Book of Living and Dying*, p. 61.*)

Cultivating mindfulness can lead to the discovery of the deep realms of energy medicine, where insight and calmness abide within a wellspring of acceptance and healing. In this particular way of paying attention, looking deeply into one's self in the kind context of a spirit of learning, one allows a process of relief of suffering and release of illusion.

Attending Now and Being, those "distinguished energies" within the practice of Reiki, are part of a *process,* one that suggests a distinct forward movement from one point or context to another, and also alludes to transformation, where we may begin to view ourselves from the standpoint of our underlying nature—from our place in a whole system, from our place in an unfolding universe. We may begin to view ourselves in the broader context of a common vision. In her book *Mahina Tiare!*,* Reiki practitioner Barbara Marrett provides an excellent metaphor for this process. Recounting the story of her sailing adventure from Friday Harbor in Puget Sound to the South Seas, she declares, "We were steering by hand, and it was all I could manage to keep the boat on course." Here is a metaphor for the *process of attending.*

Course correction, whether accomplished in a boat at sea or on an attentive "inner journey," can be challenging. It requires *mindfulness.* The ability to attend to the moment at hand is a mark of the energetically-aware person.

---

*See Appendix C, Suggested Reading

This capacity grows with practice and requires focus, ("steering by hand") which ensures that we reach our destination. In the case of the practice of Reiki, we create an opening for celebrating life, which fosters a vigilant attitude by grounding us in the physical task at hand.

How much of your experience in life takes place in the *now* moment? How much takes place in your fearful imagination—or wishful thinking? (For example, when you are brushing your teeth in the morning, are you really someplace else or are you saying to yourself, "Wow, I'm brushing my teeth, and I hope all teeth in the world are feeling as good as mine?") How much of your life is a reaction, a return to the past, or a fantasy? Try the following processes.

Try This Process: *Ki* Key ∨ a
Present Moment Staying Power

- *How's your present moment staying power?*
- *Check the boxes, and note.*
- *How much of your life is a reaction?*
- *How much is "could be" a return to the past, or a fantasy of the way through?*

Were you in the present moment when you

Opened my eyes in the morning?	❏ Yes	❏ No
Bathed?	❏ Yes	❏ No
Brushed teeth?	❏ Yes	❏ No
Exercised?	❏ Yes	❏ No
Got dressed?	❏ Yes	❏ No
Kissed someone?	❏ Yes	❏ No
Had your morning meal?	❏ Yes	❏ No
Started the day's activities?	❏ Yes	❏ No
Cared for others?	❏ Yes	❏ No
Talked with your first person?	❏ Yes	❏ No
Handled business over the phone?	❏ Yes	❏ No
Went through the day, (by the hour?)	❏ Yes	❏ No
Talked with last person?	❏ Yes	❏ No
Hugged someone?	❏ Yes	❏ No
Settled in at home?	❏ Yes	❏ No
Watered the plants?	❏ Yes	❏ No
Petted the cat, played with the dog?	❏ Yes	❏ No
Listened to music?	❏ Yes	❏ No
Practiced Reiki?	❏ Yes	❏ No
Fixed dinner?	❏ Yes	❏ No
Snuggled?	❏ Yes	❏ No

Try This Process: *Ki* Key VI b
Here and Now Percentages

Mark the boxes below with numbers representing your (1) absent (2)reactive or (3) "here and now" moments. After 21 days, tally the numbers. What percentage of your life's process is "here and now?" P.S. Give yourself a (4) for lucid dreaming.

21-Day "Here and Now" Percentages (1=absent, 2=reactive, 3=present, 4=lucid dreaming)																					
Day	1	2	3	4	5	6	7	8	9	10	11	12	13	14	15	16	17	18	19	20	21
Time 6:am																					
7																					
8																					
9																					
10																					
11																					
12																					
1:pm																					
2																					
3																					
4																					
5																					
6																					
7																					
8																					
9																					
10																					
11																					
12																					
1:am																					
2																					
3																					
4																					
5																					
Total:																					

Tally for # 1: ____ = ____ ? % of Grand Total ____

Tally for # 2: ____ = ____ ? % of Grand Total ____

Tally for # 3: ____ = ____ ? % of Grand Total ____

Tally for # 4: ____ = ____ ? % of Grand Total ____

Grand Total

*R*eiki encourages us to come in contact, in each moment, with our *experience*—and then to use this as a "ladder" to the understanding of others. In a world of dualities, of "this and that," of "self and other," the practice of Reiki allows us to touch our *experience* completely—in each present moment —while cultivating tenderness and an attitude of non-judgment, where we simply *acknowledge* things as they are.

In the practice of Reiki, we observe whatever comes up (distress, anxiety, annoyance, delight, elation, relief) without claiming it. We let it evaporate into the field of *being* without holding on to it. In this practice, which deals with a direct human experience of change and growth, we are, here and now, just *being*, looking precisely at our state of mind without trying to alter it. The practice of Reiki cultivates openness towards self, others, the environment, moment by moment, anew.

Seven Factors of Enlightment

1. Mindfulness
2. Investigation
3. Energy
4. Rapture
5. Tranquility
6. Concentration
7. Equanimity

Unfolding NOW

Doing is familiar. However, *allowing* right now (releasing the mind's distractions) and *observing* is an artscience. You may find that when you are the Observer of all that is going on in your life you release yourself from reacting to memories. Neither do you have fantasies of the future. You are just here, *Now*—in this happy timespace! You change.

Some people might think attempting to "let go" by being mindful of present moments (focused) is extremely challenging. But I have come to see that it can be found within the context of the practice of Reiki—easily found. Here, the *Ki*-Keys of *Attending Now and Being* crystallize in the interaction of an inner truth with that truth residing in the Whole. When one lives life at each moment, an organic dynamic unfolds. This is a shift towards the positive, leading to dissolved stress, and a sense of well-being in relationship to the entire synergistic system. Citing her experience throughout years of Reiki practice, Dr. Paula Horan says, "We tend to lose our addiction to intellectual explanations. Instead, we begin to live in the moment. We *experience* life at a gut level, with our immediate and spontaneous feelings [rather than] in our heads—with thoughts that divide and separate."

Indeed, mindfulness (*Attending Now and Being*) means that one can recognize oneself as separate from one's thoughts, untether one's self from projecting those thoughts upon self and others. Beyond this, by actually practicing or by participating in Reiki, you are exercising your capacity to *deliberately* alter your stance in relationship to life situations.

You do this not by shutting yourself off from the situations or by subjecting yourself to them, but by accepting, embracing *what is* with full attention, sinking into the pain and into the emptiness—or the pleasure and bliss—trusting the birth of the *new*. With this perception, you look at life's *process* and say, *"What can I learn from this?"* Thus, you create the path of your life, and carve out a space in which your unique agendas are seen for what they are, within the full range of your highest consciousness and within the full spectrum of *possibility*!

"Carving out Spaces"

Catalysts

*P*articipating in the Reiki *process* encourages not only relaxation, but the activation of certain energetic skills which you already have, but of which you may as yet be unaware. These capacities are *agents of change*. The *Ki-* Keys manifest expanded awareness. We come to see that the practice of Reiki is about learning receptivity by trusting ourselves in openness, stillness, empathy, attunement to energy, and pure potential. We do this as dual citizens of physical and energetic realms. Indeed, we can sculpt spaces, spaces of possibility, spaces full of surprise and delight, spaces bolder than any previously imagined. And, in these "Reiki spaces," we can experience ourselves, others, and our universe compassionately, because through the practice of Reiki, we become like hollow channels through which Life Energy resonates.

As a methodology, Reiki is proactive, it is a creative artform much like a duet played ensemble by practitioner and recipient, (or by practitioner and a state of relaxed optimal well-being). It *can* be a "fugue" of melodic proportion involving practitioner/recipient, cosmos, and Cosmos. Your *experience* with Reiki depends upon your willingness to enter into the "moment," into a *new* way of being.

Experience has shown that in becoming fluent in the many facets and in the artful practice of "energy medicine," the Reiki practitioner funds inner strength. Upon this you can rely. Moreover, this juicy practice opens the possibility for renewed creativity, for a transformation of consciousness. As you continue to explore, to accept, and to empower yourself, you will notice that you are able to "see" energetically as well as physically... you can now come to a mode of *being* that starts from the encompassing Whole, and then touches others (sub-wholes) in a dynamic, interconnected, holistic world beyond.

Try This Process: *Ki* Key V c
Discovering Energy Medicine

If you check yes on four or more of the items below, you're on the road to discovering energy medicine.

1. You have an energy field (HEF).   ❑ Yes   ❑ No   ❑ Maybe

2. Your soft boundaries are measurable   ❑ Yes   ❑ No   ❑ Maybe
    by modern state-of-the-art scientific
    instrumentation.

3. Your boundaries are not your physical   ❑ Yes   ❑ No   ❑ Maybe
    extremities.

4. When you are relaxed, energy flows   ❑ Yes   ❑ No   ❑ Maybe
    easily through your energy field.

5. You are capable of recognizing your own   ❑ Yes   ❑ No   ❑ Maybe
    life-force energy, and that of other living
    creatures.

6. You can refine your skills, and expand   ❑ Yes   ❑ No   ❑ Maybe
    your awareness to see the world
    in a new way; that is, energetically.

7. Through Reiki you can facilitate change,   ❑ Yes   ❑ No   ❑ Maybe
    and an unfolding to a higher order of
    consciousness.

8. You are able to empathize.   ❑ Yes   ❑ No   ❑ Maybe

9. You are able at times to "stay present"   ❑ Yes   ❑ No   ❑ Maybe
    in the present.

10. You are striving for "core" harmony.   ❑ Yes   ❑ No   ❑ Maybe

Try This Process: *Ki* Key V d
Expanding Awareness Expectations

As you move into the experience of multidimensionality and its implications,
it is wise to note your expectations.

- **Physical Expectations:**

- **Mental Expectations:**

- **Emotional Expectations:**

- **Relationship Expectations:**

- **Inner Spirit Expectations:**

- **Energetic Expectations:**

- **Global Expectations:**

How do these expectations differ from those you noted in Chapter Two?

12

The Reiki Methodology
A Participatory Model

"I held it truth, with him who sings
To one clear harp in divers tones,
That men may rise on stepping-stones
Of their dead selves to higher things."

Alfred Lord Tennyson

Anthem

We living creatures,
we felicitous fields
of patterns
of energy
of life-force energy
boundless ki,
of a limitless source;

Interconnected,
resonating,
living creatures flowing
with potential's course;
now one with the whole,
as whirlpools in a stream,

Now distinct within
the whole,
as whirlpools in a stream,
open to receive,
free to alignwith design
mystical,

Reflections of the
organizing principle,
ever present
ever magical,
we living creatures
are the fugues
of resonant being.

Wind-in-the-Feather

"If you help others, you will be helped, perhaps tomorrow, perhaps in one hundred years, but you will be helped. Nature must pay off the debt... It is a mathematical law and all life is mathematics."

~ Gurdjieff

Innate Capacities

It seems hard to find an all-inclusive answer to the question of how or why *relaxation* nurtures the desire, and can even prompt the discovery of, *whole systems* thought. Perhaps such an answer is less important than the *experience* of integration with the whole, as the *Interlude* following this chapter demonstrates. Human beings, it seems, possess the innate capacity to come into a harmonious relationship with the natural order, with Self, with Other. In exploring this relationship of interdependence and of balance, the Buddhist model, which is based upon empathic experience (and upon whose foundation Reiki rests), aims to facilitate the *experience.* Here myth and math intertwine and embrace the whole. The growing field of psychoneuroimmunology is a case in point. As they seek to establish the link between mind and body—between thoughts and the function of immune cells, scientists within this field demonstrate how conditions such as stress can negatively impact immunity. They point out, for example, how the flight-or-fight response is mediated by the nervous system, where the physiology of chronic stress can exacerbate "dis-ease." In fact, researchers have been able to show that the *way* we look at stress is significant.

"A sense sublime...
a motion and a spirit, that impells all thinking things, all objects of all thought, and rolls through all things..."

William Wordsworth

The Reiki methodology provides a venue for shifting our perceptions of stress and for coping with stress within a positive frame of reference. Reiki is not a new technology recently brought forward in response to research, but an ancient and venerable one dating back to (at least) 2600 B.C., and to certain esoteric healing practices of the Buddhist tradition—and certain insights regarding *nonlinear* experience. Within this *experience,* awareness of the everyday moments of one's life encourages a sense of inner peace. To the extent that one engages the *process* (the connections, the relationship dynamics of the whole system), one accelerates an innate capacity to heal.

If through the mirror of Reiki you were to see yourself from the wider view of "a multidimensional energetic phenomenon that resonates with a whole system," you would encounter a fresh vision of your intimate relationship to a vital force and to *Universal Life-force*. Practicing Reiki interjects energy on many levels. With this practice, you may well reinterpret events in your life as well as the significance they hold for you and how you choose to work with them. You can reorganize yourself, adjusting through focusing your mind, through quieting the mind-body, to come to an inner silence and to enter a place of stillness. You can reframe your attitudes.

Indeed, one can become absorbed in the Reiki process very comfortably, moving into places of spaciousness and possibility, becoming mindful of tension, noticing nuances of feeling and subtleties of energy flow, without judgment, allowing then releasing mind-body distress.

I made a list the other day of all the methods of "just letting go" that I could call to mind—from "A to Z": Attitude adjustment, biking, cantering through mountain valleys just after sunrise, dancing, envisioning great open spaces, etc.—all the way to Yoga and Zen gardening. I noted that all these are things you *do or learn to* do to reorient yourself, in timespace. They all "work," but Reiki, a *being* artscience, is different—unique among these.

Reiki is Different

In the first place, Reiki differs from other (relaxation) methodologies and techniques because, as a "hands-on" practice it *catalyzes* vital force, (or *Universal Life-force Energy*). Thus, the Reiki methodology distinguishes itself as *energy medicine*. More than just a "releasing" or "awareness expanding" technology, Reiki transcends the limitations of time and space. It can lead to recognition of the human self as a creature of both physical and energetic realms. The practitioner can *experience self within a multidimensional whole system.* Thus, healthful attitudinal and perceptual shifts can occur. On all levels, deep relaxation, a by-product of the Reiki practice, soothes the mind-body-inner-spirit. Yet, despite its potential for accelerating positive change, this practice is as simple and as natural as a smile on the face of your best friend.

Secondly, the Reiki methodology is different from other modern relaxation practices because its origins are very, very old. These ancient roots, along with the transmission of empowerment to students of the practice and an honorable lineage, set Reiki apart.

Reiki was rediscovered by Dr. Mikao Usui (as we have seen in Chapter Four). As recounted in that chapter, Dr. Usui had developed an increased awareness of the inner energy system and its potential for creating mind-body balance. He surely knew of certain complex esoteric practices relating to the transfer of energy. The well-guarded practices had been transmitted from master to student over the centuries for eons, but had been forgotten. As Usui rediscovered these treasures, he also reopened ancient channels of communication. These could be traced back two thousand years earlier to Gautama, the Buddha, who understood the intuitive perception of form.

Now we know that from the time of Dr. Usui's transmission of the teachings there has been an unbroken line of hand-trained teachers of Reiki. These individuals can trace their roots through one of his students. In the West, for example, we are indebted to Hawayo Takata,* a Japanese-American healer who studied Reiki in Japan over fifty years ago. Despite enormous challenges during times of international conflict, Takata transported the gift of learning to North America where the teachings took root in western consciousness. The basic Reiki instruction as taught by Takata was transmitted just as it had been from her mentors. Takata was the student of Chujiro Hayashi, one of nineteen master teachers trained by Usui himself.

---

* See Appendix A

A third way in which Reiki is different is that completion of training is celebrated with a "graduation" ceremony. Upon the completion of each training, the student is able to move beyond illusory and limiting constraints. Moving beyond the apparent, the student is able to see that our nature *is* all that we *are*. Without *being* it, this is also awareness, woven into a tapestry of interconnected processes.

As the student graduates, a shift of emphasis from object to process occurs, a shift to an inner knowing of the dynamic character of reality. There is a realization of the holistic nature of experience. This in turn leads to the understanding that there is an interplay between actuality and possibility, as students come to see their place in a coherent process within a total system, where enlightened self-interest demonstrates how we belong to ourselves, and how we belong to others.

Mastery expresses itself in the graduation ceremony called *The Ceremony of Attunement*. What happens during the ceremony has sometimes been compared with the first time someone flips the switch to light a building already wired. The Reiki Master "flips the switch," and you are "connected," consciously, with a Limitless Whole, the source of *Ki*, in a new way. This is not to say that you were not connected before—rather that your commitment, in combination with the *Ceremony*, amplifies and accelerates your awareness of *Life-force Energy* and your "plug-in points!" Teachers remind students that it is because of their commitment that they open to possibilities. It is because of their *intent* that awareness blossoms. It is by *their* contemplation that they come to see. Even though a Reiki Master, in the great tradition of *The Usui System of Reiki*, "gives the blessing" and conducts the ceremony, it is the student—through self-nuturance, and self-cultivation, not an external authority—who evokes the shift.

To be "attuned" to Reiki means to awaken *a new way of seeing*, a new way of living, and to establish a new global consciousness in which a rigid perception is replaced with celebration of Life. In this breakthrough the Whole synergistically reveals itself, and this through a special ceremony, the purpose of which is to communicate directly from one consciousness to the other, in order to manifest a transformation of consciousness, in which a change occurs— be it subtle or significant.

Therapeutic Reiki

Once a person has experienced *The Ceremony of Attunement*, that individual can expect a stronger connection with *Life-force Energy, Ki*. When one is in a state of well-being, *Ki* flows freely in, throughout, and from a living creature, in a *balanced* manner. This has a nourishing effect on all the organs of the body, as well as upon the mind, the emotions, and inner spirit. Attuned Reiki practitioners, focusing intently on supporting a state of well-being, strengthen or reconnect with Life's pulsing by approaching a calm, focused state of awareness. (Remember Reiki is a *being* practice, a life-affirming *process*.) Practitioners often are able to move beyond their immediate ego needs, thus activating an open pathway through which vital energy may flow. Now an initial intent of relaxation or tension release may also induce a quickening, or an expanding awareness of patterns of energy. Moving sequentially, from one position to the next, practitioners can *experience* a forward movement toward renewal. The Reiki methodology is a participatory one. As you prepare for a Reiki session, and as you actually *experience* it, you will probably note many responses and interactions.

Participating in a Reiki Session

*f*or those of you who are reading this book and are new to Reiki, let us say that the Reiki *experience* can be powerful. That is why it is a good idea to set aside a few moments to prepare for the Reiki Session. This preparation time is not part of the content of *The Usui System's* methodology or format, just advice from many participants/practitioners/ recipients who report that "warming-up" exercises, such as those which follow, seem to complement the session.

Warming Up

*I*n preparing for a Reiki Session, you will close your eyes, breathe deeply, and imagine a tranquil scene. Stay focused on this image until your mind and emotions are quiet and a sensation of relaxation occurs. Soon, you can feel centered, as your edges soften. The foreground of your awareness is in rhythm with the *Now*. You are in a "listening" mode, able to detect subtle cues. You remind yourself of your role in the upcoming Session. You focus intent on being present, a catalyst, conduit, or channel of *Life-force Energy*.

Directly preceding the actual Reiki Session, many participants/recipients employ the following techniques to start relaxing. They advise practicing deep breathing and focusing intent excercises (see Appendix B) in a quiet, warm space. Here you will be undisturbed. It is nice to select music appropriate for relaxation to accompany the session, and to prepare a comfortable, cushioned table and chair(s). Dim the lights to encourage the process, loosen tight clothing, take off shoes or other constricting items, and just close your eyes— mentally clear your mind of the hubbub of the day or any other distracting thoughts. Next, sweep your hands from the top of the head to the lower body, while doing an inventory/

"A guardian angel o'er his life presiding,
Doubling his pleasures,
And his cares dividing."

Samuel Rogers
Human Life

assessment of sensations—making mental notes—and alerting the body that something special is about to begin. If you are offering a session to someone else, you would, at this point, ask if there is anything to which you should direct attention. (Do this for yourself, too.) Warm-up feet and ankles by gently holding insoles, and softly manipulating the area (an old trick I learned from Joan Marie). Important: Pour a glass of water. Drink it after the Reiki Session.

Try This Process: Warming Up
Prepare for the Reiki Session in the Following Ways

relax

close eyes

imagine a tranquil scene

focus your attention there

focus intent

notice a quieting

notice a "centering"

breathe, consciously

be comfortable

come to a still point

clear mind

come to "listening mode"

inventory tense areas

gently rub feet and ankles

stay present

open to healthful, meaningful relaxation

notice a shift in pace

The Reiki Session: A Natural (Whole System) Process

*N*ow preparations for the Reiki Session are complete, and the session begins. Holding a still heart-mind-space, and intending "the highest good of all concerned," the therapist/ practitioner lightly places hands just above the recipient's eyes. A process of drawing, or transference of energy, commences. Energy flows to receptors in the mind-body-spirit in a whole systems, multidimensional *experience*. A shift occurs. You begin to relax. This may be very distinct or subtle, and relates to the energy flow. While the recipient is relaxing comfortably, the therapist/practitioner is breathing, *allowing* rather than directing the flow of energy to move through the energy field to that of the recipient, progressing through each of approximately twenty (20) positions, aligning with sequences of energetic flow, and *allowing* this to flow naturally. The recipient is being presented with a different mind-body "sense," and responds with any number of indicators that *tension* is lessening

If a person is tense or is experiencing stress-related illness or symptoms, *Ki* is out of balance. As the Reiki Session progresses, that person can draw or pull *Ki* as needed. We notice that this *process* varies in speed and intensity. Fast, slow, sporadic or constant, one continues to *draw* energy until reaching a point of "Enough." The flow stops. The universe is intelligent, and inherently knows exactly what is needed in establishing individual balance, once *Life-force energy* is activated. Next, spontaneous changes may commence. It may feel as if a whole layer of "stuff" is sloughed-off or drained away, freeing that which lies beneath —until finally, *balance* is restored, and a sense of inner peace occurs. Indeed, the practice of Reiki can accelerate the healing *process*. Imbalance that can be expressed as tension, stress, irritability, illness, pain, and discomfort clears.

The Reiki Session is an opportunity to reorchestrate one's living dynamic. It is very powerful. It is very simple.

Dr. Mari Hall
Longtime Reiki Master

"But, who can paint
Like Nature?
Can imagination boast,
Amid it's gay creation,
hues like hers?"

James Thomson
The Seasons. Spring

Reiki is not a system that promises spontaneous healing, yet you can *expect* startling therapeutic responses. If something miraculous occurs, it is imperative to remember: Reiki is the miracle-worker. We are *not doing* something, rather we are simply *being*, or *allowing* ourselves to connect with Limitless Potential in a special way—similar to the way we resonate with the special energy of a certain place. We invite *Ki* to flow through us. Both practitioner and recipient are energized in the process, but do not take on or give to others either negativity or wellness. *The Usui System of Reiki* nurtures my/our/ your deep, compassionate, empathic *intent* to be a catalyst for the highest good of all concerned from the stance of empathy, or compassion. What may *be*?…we do not know; we simply trust in the Primary Order. From here, our natural abilities to heal, transcend, and transform proceed.

Before and After

*T*he following charts attempt to describe the qualities of the subtle energy of Reiki that you may feel physically before and after a Reiki session. Poetry lends itself better to this task than does prose. If the primary colors were analogous to body sensations felt in massage, *then tones and hues* might be analogous to sensations felt in a Reiki session. Nevertheless, I hope that you will find the words, phrases, metaphors or analogies of interest, and search for some of your own. As I have said, "Reiki's energy is very mysterious!" It is hard to describe in words.

Whatever words you use to describe the sensations in your hands and body as you progress in your Reiki *experience*, know that skill and sensitivity do intensify with practice. In the final analysis, your own inner knowing far surpasses descriptive phrases. Nuances are in the realm of intuition, and a very personal thing. In our society, we express ourselves almost exclusively in words. Yet, in Reiki the *artscience*, we trust in the *process*. By allowing this openness, we give birth to inn vision, inn r wisdom, and peace of mind which touches us on all energetic levels in our physical and nonphysical being.

Before	After
Reiki practitioners' feedback regarding sensations felt in hands as session commences. These might indicate imbalance, obstruction, or depletion.	Reiki practitioners' feedback regarding sensations felt in hands during closing sweep. These might indicate balanced or revived energy.
• *Drawing* • *Pulling* • *Prickly, Hot Denseness* • *Smoggy Heaviness* • *Stuffy Pressure* • *Numb Feelings* • *Wavy Heat* • *Cold, Vacuum-Like Sensations* • *Wooly, Thick Blanket*	• *Silkiness* • *Smoothness* • *Unbrokenness* • *Softness* • *Warmth* • *Continuous, Peaceful Pulsing* • *Glowing* • *Glimmery, Expansive* • *Flowing, Even*

Interlude

"A still mind is one that is free from fear, from fantasies, free from ruminations over the past, free from concern about what may or may not be happening to it.

Peter Russell
The White Hole in Time

Interludes

Affirmations,
Thanksgivings,
Ecstasies...

Deeply felt
Deeply shareable
Journeys of Life

Journeys
of Healing Power

Wind-in-the-Feather

"You deserve a break today..."

~ Advertising jingle

An Interlude: The Reiki Break

*T*he notion of "taking time out" to enjoy life spurs the economy. Everywhere advertisements remind consumers of the benefits to be derived in the pursuit of family and personal enjoyment. The *"You deserve a break today..."* advertising jingle probably is just as well known in some parts of the world as are the opening bars of *Beethoven's Fifth!* Obviously, the phrase "You deserve a break today..." touches home. We do deserve a break, for creative play, for healthful living.

Before we begin *Part Two,* where we will examine practical ways for connecting with revitalizing *Life-force energy*, let's sample the kind of "time out" a growing number of Reiki practitioners recommend.

Let's take a Reiki Break.

"Some feelings
are to mortals given,
With less of earth in them,
than heaven."

Sir Walter Scott
Lay of the Last Minstrel

The Reiki Break

The *Reiki Break* is a favorite of many practitioners and recipients of Reiki. It is a planned pause during which you set out to consider, to focus on, and to relish the possibilities *in* the moment and *of* the moments of your Life. Perhaps that is why many individuals have come to regard the *Reiki Break* as an inspired intervention for relaxation. After all, you need not be a Reiki practitioner to *experience* the shift that occurs as this time-out strengthens coping mechanisms.

With the aforementioned pluses, why not just set out for a sunset ride, or plan a daily adjournment to your favorite soaking tub? Good ideas, but the *Reiki Break* offers you more. In this relaxing interlude, you may come to regard the world as *present*—in the moment. You may focus your intention towards preventative care. You may attend to chronic or acute situations. You may facilitate the filtering out of fearful resistance to what is before you and the formation of any number of possibilities. There is bounty in a *Reiki Break*.

If you are willing to set aside fifteen or twenty minutes, once or twice a day, you can touch base with your own multidimensional self. You can engage the *process* of creative fueling, placing yourself in a timespace where exists a qualitative oneness with Nature and Life.

If that is your wish, and if you would like a direct **experience** of what can happen when you take a *Reiki Break*, please try *The 7-Day Reiki Break Time Shifter* that follows. See how you like stepping beyond the restrictive confines of your normal control patterns and routine.

The 7-Day Reiki Break Time-Shifter

I invite you now to join me at my favorite imaginary spa, where we will just relax into the moment at hand in a location not found on any map. Directions leading you to this little treasure follow. There is a regimen also, and it can benefit you in these ways:

- It can help you redirect your attention towards the possibilities of the moment.

- It can remind you to focus on honoring your legitimate need to replenish your multidimensional self, on a regular basis.

- It can be a valuable tool for insight into creative and transformational energy.

As you begin *The 7-Day Reiki Break Time-Shifter Interlude* you will find yourself seeing things in new ways, visiting life in new ways. You may rediscover your native capacity for well-being. You may get back in touch with your love of life and celebrate your place in the entirety of it. Certainly, you already have the tools to do this. At the end of your week, perhaps you will have found new connections with abundant energy. You may delight in feeling very relaxed and together and your admirers may smile at the becoming twinkle in your eyes.

Journal

The 7-Day Reiki Break
Time-Shifter Interlude

Day 1: You have heard the story of Mikao Usui. Take a 10-minute time-out for a walk in Nature while you reflect upon what this story tells you that is relevant in your life. Note your thoughts.

Day 2: Take a personal time out. Find an object that reminds you of what is important to you in the story of Usui. (Try to do this on a walk in Nature). Sit with this talisman, using it as an anchor as you imagine drawing upon the creative, revitalizing juices of the cosmos.

Day 3: This is a 15-minute break. Think about the Usui story as you relax alone in a quiet space. If you cannot fast for 21 days, what would be a good starting place for you? Make yourself a promise to start—wherever that may be. Next, schedule a time for contemplation.

Day 4: Find one more focusing object. Use this to represent your commitment to yourself to incorporate self-nurturing, creative, and transformative actions into your everyday routine. Now (very important) assign this object the task of signaling your mind-body to relax quickly into a space so vast virtually anything might happen.

Days 5, 6, and 7: Begin this time-shifter by exhaling and inhaling for a brief period; slowly and consciously breathing out, counting to an even count (I suggest no more than eight) then breathing in. Seat yourself in an erect, but comfortable posture with eyes on your chosen focusing object, remembering its task from Day 4.

Days 5, 6, and 7 continued...

Journal

Now, breathing out... all the air out of your lungs... push it all out... *then taking a deep, cleansing breath in...* slowly, to the same count, commence your time-out and a sense of spacious relaxation.

Each day go to a quiet space. This may be outside or inside.

Continue the practice each day of breathing out and in; letting the breath come, paying attention to your breathing until you sense a *shift*.

You are noticing (each day) your thoughts and letting them just float by, and you are now able to feel very relaxed as you continue.

Fold your hands over your heart as you visualize all the stresses and strains you have encountered this day dissolving as if they were part of a fluid stream of clouds dusting by your heart space, and leaving it refreshed.

Imagine a crystal seed in solution growing larger and more complex. See yourself now as a seed in dynamic complexity becoming ordered and in harmony with your "best self."

Open, and *experience* the flow of restorative energy, cascading down from the crown of your head, into the places below... reorganizing, re-establishing balance, and replenishing as it streams... bringing you increased awareness of energetic momentum.

Try This Process: New Perspectives
A. Patterns of Tension or Distress

Each day review from your calm space ways in which to cope with difficult situations, resolve sticky issues and relationships, and release stress.

Your New Perspectives Regarding Patterns:

Day 1. Physical:

Day 2. Mental:

Day 3. Emotional:

Day 4. Relationship:

Day 5. Inner Spirit:

Day 6. Workplace:

Day 7. World/Local Community:

Try This Process: New Perspectives
B. Opportunities to Self-Actuate

Relaxing into yourself means being "in intregrity" with yourself, releasing life strategies that are self-defeating or unfulfilling. During this 7-day process investigate ways in which you can live up to your own potential.

<u>Your New Perspectives Regarding Opportunities</u>:

Day 1. Physical:

Day 2. Mental:

Day 3. Emotional:

Day 4. Relationship:

Day 5. Inner Spirit:

Day 6. Workplace:

Day 7. World/Local Community:

Try This Process: New Perspectives
c. Healing the Global Community

As you enjoy an inner peace, what can this mean in each of the areas below with regard to your contribution to global well-being and to cultivating openness towards self, others, and the environment?

<u>**Patterns of tension or distress I see:**</u>

Day 1. Physical:

Day 2. Mental:

Day 3. Emotional:

Day 4. Relationship:

Day 5. Inner Spirit:

Day 6. Community:

Day 7. World/Local Community:

The universe in which we all live is alive! It is a living, breathing energy system of which everything in existence is a part and interconnected.

Most of us, without thinking, believe that our bodies and our surroundings are solid; however, the latest developments in physics have shown that "the body human" and all other objects are composed of living energy. Vast levels of experiments have shown our interconnectedness and our relational aspect as being part of the whole of the universe—and of each other. Therefore, it follows that what affects one affects all.

The Reiki methodology is an ancient art form that allows the individual to tap into the universal energies of "at-ONE-ment."

part two: application

13

Participatory Themes: Focusing Intent Practice

'hunt half a day for a forgotten dream.'

William Wordsworth

Energy
patterns
of the universe
renewed,
transformed
by soft lightspheres
eternally
burning
in petal-like forms
emanating,
perfuming
the midnight sky
with the
essence of rose,
pass through the terraces
of the searcher's
mindful repose
to a primordial
mystic world
glowing,
in Reverse.

Wind-in-the-Feather

"Beware when the great God lets loose a thinker on this planet. Then all things are at risk. It is as when a conflagration has broken out in a great city, and no man knows what is safe, or where it will end."

~ *Ralph Waldo Emerson*

Participating

*P*articipating in, and therefore *experiencing*, tells more than all the words the pen can write. Experience is knowing, knowing we can ameliorate damages, knowing we can find the energetic space to treat distress and disease within ourselves (and correct toxicity in our world). Our destinies are interwoven with the workings of Nature. We can come to see how "cosmic breath" supports our survival as a living global community. Because the practice of Reiki can lead us to experience a knowing of a transcendent, unitive state, it is transformative. The Reiki *experience* can manifest the wholeness of our nature, in which distressed parts are just a matter of relativity. We, body-mind and inner spirit, our global village, our land and seas and skies, in balance and harmony, can resonate together. There is only the question: Are we enterprising enough to reorient our thinking, to learn ways to express ourselves appropriately just one degree beyond the norm?

"The meaning of things
lies not in the things themselves,
but in our attitude towards them."

Antoine de Saint Exupery

**Try This Process:
How to Use
Focusing Intent Exercises**

Journal

What to Do:	
• Read this entire section	
• Familiarize yourself with statements of intent	
• Follow the examples of methodology	
• Relax. Breathe.	
• Focus intent	
• Pay attention to shifts and awareness	
• Allow spacetime	
• Reflect	
• Record	

Focusing Intent Exercises

*7*he following section (designed to be used by Reiki practitioners and by those interested in Reiki) contains thematic exercises, participatory opportunities, and a method for *experiencing* anew. Here you will find typical examples of the potential for change available in a Reiki session. You will also find comments from a number of recipients which are included here to demonstrate what can happen when you access your innate healing capacities.

To use this section: First, read the entire section carefully. Familiarize yourself with the *Statements of Intent* and with the examples of methodology provided. Now you are ready to consider *Theme One*.

In *Theme One* (and *Two, Three, Four, Five*): Follow the example, or establish, define, and write your statement of intent. Now proceed to the application, either following the example, or inserting specifics as you desire. Relax. Breathe. Focus your intent and begin. Pay attention to shifts in awareness (be they subtle or intense) as you move into and through the exercise. Allow 5 - 10 minutes per exercise.

After each exercise, reflect on the *multidimensional* aspects of your experiences, feelings, revelations, as well as any lessons which may have come to you. Record your new seeing, new hearing, and share with yourself a new wisdom, a new "voice," a fuller sense of connectedness to the Universe.

"Sweet Memory!
wafted by thy gentle gale.
Oft up the stream of Time,
I turn my sail."

Samuel Rogers
The Pleasures of Memory

Focusing Intent Exercises

Theme One Impressions

"I felt relieved. I had my hands over my eyes. Quickly I found a "safe place," and I was able to look at things more calmly from this place. Tension lifted."

~ J.T.

"Colors shot up against darkness—a neon lime green, a brilliant blue, and this inspired a painting."

~ A.S.

"My perception of the world changed."

~ C.H.

Focusing Intent Exercises

Theme One: Eyes
Hands, fingers, and thumbs held together are brought to rest just over, but not touching, the eyes.

Statement of Intent: (*Example*) It is my intent to gain a new perspective (vision) on the issue of understanding another person's point of view (eyes). In the past, it has been hard for me to see through another's eyes, which has helped to create tension in my life.

Method: (*Example*) Put your hands over your eyes. Breathe, get comfortable, and then "look at" a conversation you had recently, in which you came to understand or had an opportunity to understand someone else *in a new way.* Allow yourself to be in a state of relaxed alertness, quiet but focused. "Look at" the environment and *see* again this situation. Take note of the other person's eyes, and their expressions during the conversation. Focus your *intent*, which is to bring even more energy (*Ki*), to an inner vision supporting empathy and strong communication.

Your Statement of Intent:

Your Method: (as above, or...)

journal

Theme Two
Impressions

"When I was a little kid and I was waiting upstairs for Santa to come, I thought I heard a noise downstairs and my whole body 'listened.' It was as if I tuned in my ears to hear a whisper. That's what happened again with this session."

~ M.H.

"I have a problem with clenching my teeth. My wife says I grind them loudly in my sleep. I decided to concentrate on this (second) exercise for three weeks, twice a day. I do it in the morning and just before bed. My jaw feels more relaxed, and so does my wife."

~ R.K.

Theme Two: Ears
Hands are gently drawn to sides of the head to rest on either ear and cover the jaw area, both joint and bone.

Statement of Intent: It is my intent to *listen* carefully and focus upon what I can *hear* that I might not *hear* when I am not paying attention. I would like to *hear* in a different way. (*Example*) It is my intent to *hear* again (ears) the merry sounds of playfulness. I want to bring this into conscious "inner hearing" for my co-workers, and share it at home.

Method: (*Example*) Place your hands upon your ears, and "listen" to a remembered childhood scene. Maybe you will hear the sounds of delight as kids play hide-and-seek, or maybe their yelps of surprise at some new discovery. Let your ears be attuned to the quiet and alert to those moments of stillness and anticipation we so often hide from each other. Again, trying not to burst with laughter, hear again this incredible energy the way you did when you were a child. Remember and " be" with the exhilaration as you *experience* it. Ask yourself how you might transfer the *experience*, and that same delight, to the present.

Your Statement of Intent:

Your Method: (as above, or...)

journal

Focusing Intent Exercises

Theme Three: Occipital Lobes
Hands move to back of head where they are now placed under it at the base of the skull. Keep thumbs closed into other fingers. Cradle back of head in palms.

Statement of Intent: (*Example*) It is my intent to make an energetic connection with other members of the living global community through experiencing them in new ways.

Method: (*Example*) Exhaling and inhaling gently and effortlessly, place hands as directed above. Relax into an imaginary cushion of unconditional acceptance within Mother Nature's arms. Rest in this space. Sense a timeless, floating sensation, as your life-force energy merges with that which surrounds you, extending further and further away, even to the distant stars, or to the trees of an ancient forest. Find an image that attracts you. Mentally ask permission to enter the space of another living being or natural scene. Feel the special energy of that moment, place, or natural wonder. Note that Nature vibrates with *Life-force Energy*, of which you are a part.

Your Statement of Intent:

Your Method: (as above, or...)

journal

Focusing Intent Exercises

**Theme Four: Crown
Right hand on the crown of head, left hand circles neck at base of skull.**

Statement of Intent: (*Example*) It is my intention to get in touch with my inner wisdom.

Method: (*Example*) Mentally connecting with the collective unconscious of all other sentient beings, place your hands as directed above. Make yourself accessible to whatever aspects of shared inner wisdom emerge. Trust that your highest self will assist and bring vigor to your efforts. Become mindful of expanding in a whole system of limitless possibility. Focus upon getting in touch with your own potential within that system. *Know* yourself in an energetic sense. You are in *process....*

Your Statement of Intent:

Your Method: (as above, or...)

journal

Focusing Intent Exercises

Theme Five
Impressions

"I called my old friend Ann today to ask her if she'd feel comfortable doing a Reiki session even though my throat was very sore and I had a temperature. She gave me the green light so we met. She asked me how things were going for me with my new boss. Was everything else, except my throat, O.K.?

"I shut down. I didn't want to talk about the changes going on at work, and how sales quotas and commissions were messing with my peace of mind, so she started, but when her hands were above my throat, I began to clear my throat repeatedly and to swallow over and over, real hard. And then the pain turned fuzzy.

"Afterwards, we talked about how I felt (much better). The physical improvement was not all that happened. I could also tell my friend how stressful things were at work."

~ A.W.

Theme Five: Throat

Hands float over throat area, one set of fingers atop the other, just beneath chin and above collar bones. Thumbs in.

Statement of Intent: (*Example*) It is my intent to boost my capacity to communicate clearly (throat) and positively, and thereby to lessen the tension that arises from misunderstandings.

Method: (*Example*) Breathe deeply and achieve a state of relaxation. Then, placing your hands as described above, draw energy to the intention to become naturally eloquent. *Be* with this energy, and *know* your ability to communicate fluently. Imagine yourself in lively, informative, and beneficial conversations. Feel yourself speak with conviction and confidence, the words flowing smoothly from your heart, your throat a vessel.

Your Statement of Intent:

Your Method: (as above, or...)

SoundShotStudios

"Experiencing is knowing...."

14

Relax, Open, Celebrate!
A 21-Day Process for
Reiki and Relaxation

"We know the truth, not only by the reason, but also by the heart."

Blaise Pascal

Unbroken Wholeness

Coming out of Elsewhere,
as we do -
To fogs and bogs
and city blues,
Stepping into Somewhere,
as we do -
Into a place, and into Time,
Some think we're but fragments, far
and few -
Shards, with a prismatic view,
By heaven's winds
blown all askew,
Dismembered bits, of different hues,
And risk, in all that ballyhoo,
A sense of Life, Divine.

Wind-in-the-Feather

"When I talk of letting go of ego or letting go of knowing one is unique...I am not talking of cutting oneself off from self. In fact, I am talking of befriending the deeper self within us, of befriending our passions, our deepest feelings of ecstasy and of pain."

~ Matthew Fox

The 21-Day Process for
Reiki and Relaxation

*Y*ou have just completed practice in Focusing Intent. If you are ready for the next step, which includes *experiencing* a shift in your awareness, then designate 21 days for your personal journey into the multidimensional arena of well-being. Your expedition centers on a consistent practice of relaxation and focusing exercises in combination with Reiki, and journaling. It requires commitment.

"Thus far,
we run before the wind."

Arthur Murphy
The Apprentice

You do not need to be a trained Reiki practitioner to participate in this *21-Day Process* (although Reiki I and Reiki II Training have been proven to accelerate the process); you do need an appreciation of the synergistic energetic keys (Chapters 6-11) and your focused intent for relaxing into balance within a whole system. With this in mind, you may find the *process* and exercises which follow to be an effective way in which you can develop your sense of the harmonious coherent state which the *21-Day Process* encourages.

This process, modeled on the example of Dr. Mikao Usui's personal vision quest on Mt. Kurama (Chapter 4) sets the stage for integrating a creative and life-affirming artscience into your daily routine. The *process* has two working parts.

One: Before the daily Reiki session (either as a practitioner or participant), *focus your intent*. Two: Be consistent in the practice, and keep track of what is going on each day by jotting down intent memos/notes/journal entries before and soon after each Reiki Session.

Note: If you are going to participate in the 21-Day Reiki and Relaxation Process as a Reiki recipient, be sure to schedule your sessions with the Reiki therapist in advance.

With these simple requirements understood, let's begin the *21-Day Relaxation Process* by turning our attention to how to participate in this process with "Step One: Focal Points." Focal points serve to focus attention upon areas which provide structure during the *21-Day Process*. Before starting the program, you need to review each of these feedback mechanisms, and reflect upon them as did Dr. Usui prior to his journey to Mt. Kurama. Turn now to Step One to commence the process.

Reflect on your response to the seven following focal points. Then write at least three focusing intent statements for each focal point. You will be using these later when you will make statements of intent.

I. Focal Point: The Wisdom of the Elders

If you could talk with the great awakened geniuses of the world, what would they advise you about relaxing as it relates to your well-being in the interconnected multidimensional realm of energy medicine? (Fill in your focusing intent statements below.)

-

-

-

II. Focal Point: Visualization

If you were able to relax into an empathic resonance with yourself, your family, co-workers, community, the rest of the world, and the whole of nature, how would you visualize this occurring? (Fill in your focusing intent statements below.)

-

-

-

III. Focal Point: Self-Inventory

If you were to assess your own multidimensional aspects (that is, your physical, mental, emotional relationship, spiritual, and energetic aspects) as catalysts in an ongoing relaxation practice, what would attract your attention? (Fill in your focusing intent statements below.)

·

·

·

IV. Focal Point: Awareness

If you were to consider how dissolving tension can bring you greater present-moment awareness, what would you discover, and how would you process these discoveries? (Fill in your focusing intent statements below.)

·

·

·

V. Focal Point: Sensory Awareness

If you were to examine what your physicality tells you about how life-force energy, *Ki,* works in alleviating stress in your life and how this relates to mind-body interactions, what would you find? (Fill in your focusing intent statements below.)

·

·

·

VI. Focal Point: Harmonious-Coherent States

When you are most likely to be in harmony with your inner truth, your Core self? How does this relate to relaxation? (Fill in your focusing intent statements below.)

•

•

•

VII. Focal Point: Empathy

When are you most in harmony with others and with the living global community and the natural order? How does this relate to an ongoing relaxation practice? (Fill in your focusing intent statements below.)

•

•

•

Try This Process:
Step Two, Establishing Focus

Further reflect on your response to the seven previous focal points. Then write at least three focusing intent statements for each focal point. You will use these later when you make statements of intent.

• First, select one or two areas of your mind-body on which you will be practicing tension release during the *Reiki Relaxation Session.* Remember you will be treating this area on multidimensional levels using the area of the body as a key to express your focus. (Example: if you pick eyes, then the level of "mind," you could express your focus as "creative vision." Underline these as shown on the form on page 249.)

• Next, select any one of your statements of focused intent from "Step One: Focal Points" and insert it as is appropriate in the "Statement of Intent" section, and fill in the rest of the form on page 250, as in the example on the following page.

"How To" Example:
Try This Process: Focusing Intent
21-Day Reiki and Relaxation Process

Day One: *(Example)* *Tired, irritated eyes*
(fill in area of tension release)

Statement of Intent: Using Focal Point I (Wisdom of the Elders), *it is my intent to release tension around my eyes, and to see things in new ways... to draw energy to the intent to view challenges anew while releasing physical barriers, as the great adepts throughout history might have.*

Mind: *Accelerated creative vision for enlivening work tasks.*

Body: *Relaxed eye muscles.*

Emotions: *"Seeing" different viewpoints to create a lessening of tension between family members.*

Inner Spirit: *Breathe into a visionary spirit for a new global perspective and peace in the world.*

Energetics: *Looking through the "eyes of compassion" to release anger on multidimensional levels.*

Special Challenge: *Release outmoded viewpoints for tension relief on emotional and familial scenes.*

Try This Process: Focusing Intent
21-Day Reiki and Relaxation Process

- *Select an area of tension as it is expressing itself in your physical body.*
- *Write that area of concern in the section entitled Day _____.*
- *Select a "statement of focused intent" from the "Step One: Focal Point" exercise.*
- *Fill this in below in "Statement of Intent."*
- *Complete this page as per the directions.*
- *Participate in your Reiki session.*
- *Journal your responses in the space provided.*

Day One: *(fill in area of tension release)*

Statement of Intent:

Mind:

Body:

Emotions:

Inner Spirit:

Special Challenge:

Try This Process: Focusing Intent
21-Day Reiki and Relaxation Process

- *Select an area of tension as it is expressing itself in your physical body.*
- *Write that area of concern in the section entitled Day _____.*
- *Select a "statement of focused intent" from the "Step One: Focal Point" exercise.*
- *Fill this in below in "Statement of Intent."*
- *Complete this page as per the directions.*
- *Participate in your Reiki session.*
- *Journal your responses in the space provided.*

Day Two: *(fill in area of tension release)*

Statement of Intent:

Mind:

Body:

Emotions:

Inner Spirit:

Special Challenge:

Try This Process: Focusing Intent
21-Day Reiki and Relaxation Process

- Select an area of tension as it is expressing itself in your physical body.
- Write that area of concern in the section entitled Day _____.
- Select a "statement of focused intent" from the "Step One: Focal Point: exercise.
- Fill this in below in "Statement of Intent."
- Complete this page as per the directions.
- Participate in your Reiki session.
- Journal your responses in the space provided.

Day Three: *(fill in area of tension release)*

Statement of Intent:

Mind:

Body:

Emotions:

Inner Spirit:

Special Challenge:

Journal

Try This Process: Focusing Intent
21-Day Reiki and Relaxation Process

- *Select an area of tension as it is expressing itself in your physical body.*
- *Write that area of concern in the section entitled Day _____.*
- *Select a "statement of focused intent" from the "Step One: Focal Point" exercise.*
- *Fill this in below in "Statement of Intent."*
- *Complete this page as per the directions.*
- *Participate in your Reiki session.*
- *Journal your responses in the space provided.*

Day Four: *(fill in area of tension release)*

Statement of Intent:

Mind:

Body:

Emotions:

Inner Spirit:

Special Challenge:

Try This Process: Focusing Intent
21-Day Reiki and Relaxation Process

- Select an area of tension as it is expressing itself in your physical body.
- Write that area of concern in the section entitled Day _____.
- Select a "statement of focused intent" from the "Step One: Focal Point" exercise.
- Fill this in below in "Statement of Intent."
- Complete this page as per the directions.
- Participate in your Reiki session.
- Journal your responses in the space provided.

Day Five: *(fill in area of tension release)*

Statement of Intent:

Mind:

Body:

Emotions:

Inner Spirit:

Special Challenge:

Try This Process: Focusing Intent
21-Day Reiki and Relaxation Process

- *Select an area of tension as it is expressing itself in your physical body.*
- *Write that area of concern in the section entitled Day _____.*
- *Select a "statement of focused intent" from the "Step One: Focal Point" exercise.*
- *Fill this in below in "Statement of Intent."*
- *Complete this page as per the directions.*
- *Participate in your Reiki session.*
- *Journal your responses in the space provided.*

Day Six: *(fill in area of tension release)*

Statement of Intent:

Mind:

Body:

Emotions:

Inner Spirit:

Special Challenge:

Journal

Try This Process: Focusing Intent
21-Day Reiki and Relaxation Process

- *Select an area of tension as it is expressing itself in your physical body.*
- *Write that area of concern in the section entitled Day _____.*
- *Select a "statement of focused intent" from the "Step One: Focal Point" exercise.*
- *Fill this in below in "Statement of Intent."*
- *Complete this page as per the directions.*
- *Participate in your Reiki session.*
- *Journal your responses in the space provided.*

Day Seven: *(fill in area of tension release)*

Statement of Intent:

Mind:

Body:

Emotions:

Inner Spirit:

Special Challenge:

Journal

Overview, Days 1-7
Releasing Tension

Dates: _____

Journal

Using color, shade in the columns below for the amount of tension release in each category. Observe tension release over the last 7-day period. Record for review now and at the close of the 21-day process.

Mind	Body	Emotions	Inner Spirit
10	10	10	10
9	9	9	9
8	8	8	8
7	7	7	7
6	6	6	6
5	5	5	5
4	4	4	4
3	3	3	3
2	2	2	2
1	1	1	1

10 = High Tension
1 = Low Tension

21-Day Reiki and Relaxation Process Tracking Chart for Days 1-7

Place a ✓mark at moments when you feel something significant occurred. Make sure you note this occasion in your journal.

	Sun	Mon	Tues	Wed	Thurs	Fri	Sat	
Day/Date								
A.M. ✓ / ✓ P.M.	A.M. / P.M.	A.M. / P.M.	A.M. / P.M.	A.M. / P.M.	A.M. / P.M.	A.M. / P.M.	A.M. / P.M.	◈
1								
2								
3								
4								
5								
6								
7								
8								
9								
10								
11								
12								

Try This Process: Focusing Intent
21-Day Reiki and Relaxation Process

- *Select an area of tension as it is expressing itself in your physical body.*
- *Write that area of concern in the section entitled Day _____.*
- *Select a "statement of focused intent" from the "Step One: Focal Point:" exercise.*
- *Fill this in below in "Statement of Intent."*
- *Complete this page as per the directions.*
- *Participate in your Reiki session.*
- *Journal your responses in the space provided.*

Day Eight: *(fill in area of tension release)*

Statement of Intent:

Mind:

Body:

Emotions:

Inner Spirit:

Special Challenge:

Journal

Try This Process: Focusing Intent
21-Day Reiki and Relaxation Process

- *Select an area of tension as it is expressing itself in your physical body.*
- *Write that area of concern in the section entitled Day _____.*
- *Select a "statement of focused intent" from the "Step One: Focal Point" exercise.*
- *Fill this in below in "Statement of Intent."*
- *Complete this page as per the directions.*
- *Participate in your Reiki session.*
- *Journal your responses in the space provided.*

Day Nine: *(fill in area of tension release)*

Statement of Intent:

Mind:

Body:

Emotions:

Inner Spirit:

Special Challenge:

Try This Process: Focusing Intent
21-Day Reiki and Relaxation Process

- Select an area of tension as it is expressing itself in your physical body.
- Write that area of concern in the section entitled Day _____.
- Select a "statement of focused intent" from the "Step One: Focal Point" exercise.
- Fill this in below in "Statement of Intent."
- Complete this page as per the directions.
- Participate in your Reiki session.
- Journal your responses in the space provided.

Day Ten: *(fill in area of tension release)*

Statement of Intent:

Mind:

Body:

Emotions:

Inner Spirit:

Special Challenge:

Try This Process: Focusing Intent
21-Day Reiki and Relaxation Process

Day Eleven: *(fill in area of tension release)*

Statement of Intent:

Mind:

Body:

Emotions:

Inner Spirit:

Special Challenge:

Try This Process: Focusing Intent
21-Day Reiki and Relaxation Process

- Select an area of tension as it is expressing itself in your physical body.
- Write that area of concern in the section entitled Day _____.
- Select a "statement of focused intent" from the "Step One: Focal Point" exercise.
- Fill this in below in "Statement of Intent."
- Complete this page as per the directions.
- Participate in your Reiki session.
- Journal your responses in the space provided.

Day Twelve: *(fill in area of tension release)*

Statement of Intent:

Mind:

Body:

Emotions:

Inner Spirit:

Special Challenge:

Journal

Try This Process: Focusing Intent
21-Day Reiki and Relaxation Process

- *Select an area of tension as it is expressing itself in your physical body.*
- *Write that area of concern in the section entitled Day _____.*
- *Select a "statement of focused intent" from the "Step One: Focal Point" exercise.*
- *Fill this in below in "Statement of Intent."*
- *Complete this page as per the directions.*
- *Participate in your Reiki session.*
- *Journal your responses in the space provided.*

Day Thirteen: *(fill in area of tension release)*

Statement of Intent:

Mind:

Body:

Emotions:

Inner Spirit:

Special Challenge:

Try This Process: Focusing Intent
21-Day Reiki and Relaxation Process

- *Select an area of tension as it is expressing itself in your physical body.*
- *Write that area of concern in the section entitled Day _____.*
- *Select a "statement of focused intent" from the "Step One: Focal Point" exercise.*
- *Fill this in below in "Statement of Intent."*
- *Complete this page as per the directions.*
- *Participate in your Reiki session.*
- *Journal your responses in the space provided.*

Day Fourteen: *(fill in area of tension release)*

Statement of Intent:

Mind:

Body:

Emotions:

Inner Spirit:

Special Challenge:

Overview, Days 8–14
Releasing Tension

Dates: _____

Journal

Using color, shade in the columns below for the amount of tension release in each category. Observe tension release over the last 7-day period. Record for review now and at the close of the 21-day process.

Mind	Body	Emotions	Inner Spirit
10	10	10	10
9	9	9	9
8	8	8	8
7	7	7	7
6	6	6	6
5	5	5	5
4	4	4	4
3	3	3	3
2	2	2	2
1	1	1	1

10 = High Tension
1 = Low Tension

21-Day Reiki and Relaxation Process Tracking Chart for Days 8-14

Place a ✓ mark at moments when you feel something significant occurred. Make sure you note this occasion in your journal.

	Day/Date							
	Sun	Mon	Tues	Wed	Thurs	Fri	Sat	
A.M. ✓/✓ P.M.	A.M. / P.M.	A.M. / P.M.	A.M. / P.M.	A.M. / P.M.	A.M. / P.M.	A.M. / P.M.	A.M. / P.M.	❖
1								
2								
3								
4								
5								
6								
7								
8								
9								
10								
11								
12								

Try This Process: Focusing Intent
21-Day Reiki and Relaxation Process

- *Select an area of tension as it is expressing itself in your physical body.*
- *Write that area of concern in the section entitled Day _____.*
- *Select a "statement of focused intent" from the "Step One: Focal Point" exercise.*
- *Fill this in below in "Statement of Intent."*
- *Complete this page as per the directions.*
- *Participate in your Reiki session.*
- *Journal your responses in the space provided.*

Day Fifteen: *(fill in area of tension release)*

Statement of Intent:

Mind:

Body:

Emotions:

Inner Spirit:

Special Challenge:

Try This Process: Focusing Intent
21-Day Reiki and Relaxation Process

- *Select an area of tension as it is expressing itself in your physical body.*
- *Write that area of concern in the section entitled Day _____.*
- *Select a "statement of focused intent" from the "Step One: Focal Point" exercise.*
- *Fill this in below in "Statement of Intent."*
- *Complete this page as per the directions.*
- *Participate in your Reiki session.*
- *Journal your responses in the space provided.*

Day Sixteen: *(fill in area of tension release)*

Statement of Intent:

Mind:

Body:

Emotions:

Inner Spirit:

Special Challenge:

Try This Process: Focusing Intent
21-Day Reiki and Relaxation Process

- *Select an area of tension as it is expressing itself in your physical body.*
- *Write that area of concern in the section entitled Day _____.*
- *Select a "statement of focused intent" from the "Step One: Focal Point" exercise.*
- *Fill this in below in "Statement of Intent."*
- *Complete this page as per the directions.*
- *Participate in your Reiki session.*
- *Journal your responses in the space provided.*

Day Seventeen: *(fill in area of tension release)*

Statement of Intent:

Mind:

Body:

Emotions:

Inner Spirit:

Special Challenge:

Try This Process: Focusing Intent
21-Day Reiki and Relaxation Process

- *Select an area of tension as it is expressing itself in your physical body.*
- *Write that area of concern in the section entitled Day _____.*
- *Select a "statement of focused intent" from the "Step One: Focal Point" exercise.*
- *Fill this in below in "Statement of Intent."*
- *Complete this page as per the directions.*
- *Participate in your Reiki session.*
- *Journal your responses in the space provided.*

Day Eighteen: *(fill in area of tension release)*

Statement of Intent:

Mind:

Body:

Emotions:

Inner Spirit:

Special Challenge:

Try This Process: Focusing Intent
21-Day Reiki and Relaxation Process

* *Select an area of tension as it is expressing itself in your physical body.*
* *Write that area of concern in the section entitled Day _____.*
* *Select a "statement of focused intent" from the "Step One: Focal Point" exercise.*
* *Fill this in below in "Statement of Intent."*
* *Complete this page as per the directions.*
* *Participate in your Reiki session.*
* *Journal your responses in the space provided.*

Day Nineteen: *(fill in area of tension release)*

Statement of Intent:

Mind:

Body:

Emotions:

Inner Spirit:

Special Challenge:

Journal

Try This Process: Focusing Intent
21-Day Reiki and Relaxation Process

- *Select an area of tension as it is expressing itself in your physical body.*
- *Write that area of concern in the section entitled Day _____.*
- *Select a "statement of focused intent" from the "Step One: Focal Point" exercise*
- *Fill this in below in "Statement of Intent."*
- *Complete this page as per the directions.*
- *Participate in your Reiki session.*
- *Journal your responses in the space provided.*

Day Twenty: *(fill in area of tension release)*

Statement of Intent:

Mind:

Body:

Emotions:

Inner Spirit:

Special Challenge:

Journal

Try This Process: Focusing Intent
21-Day Reiki and Relaxation Process

- Select an area of tension as it is expressing itself in your physical body.
- Write that area of concern in the section entitled Day _____.
- Select a "statement of focused intent" from the "Step One: Focal Point" exercise.
- Fill this in below in "Statement of Intent."
- Complete this page as per the directions.
- Participate in your Reiki session.
- Journal your responses in the space provided.

Day Twenty-one: *(fill in area of tension release)*

Statement of Intent:

Mind:

Body:

Emotions:

Inner Spirit:

Special Challenge:

Journal

Overview, Days 15–21
Releasing Tension

Dates: _____

Journal

Using color, shade in the columns below for the amount of tension release in each category. Observe tension release over the last 7-day period. Record for review now and at the close of the 21-day process.

Mind	Body	Emotions	Inner Spirit
10	10	10	10
9	9	9	9
8	8	8	8
7	7	7	7
6	6	6	6
5	5	5	5
4	4	4	4
3	3	3	3
2	2	2	2
1	1	1	1

10 = High Tension
1 = Low Tension

21-Day Reiki and Relaxation Process Tracking Chart for Days 15-21

Place a ✓ mark at moments when you feel something significant occurred. Make sure you note this occasion in your journal.

	Sun	Mon	Tues	Wed	Thurs	Fri	Sat	
Day/Date								
A.M. ✓ / P.M. ✓	A.M. / P.M.	A.M. / P.M.	A.M. / P.M.	A.M. / P.M.	A.M. / P.M.	A.M. / P.M.	A.M. / P.M.	◈
1								
2								
3								
4								
5								
6								
7								
8								
9								
10								
11								
12								

Three Bows and Ten Thousand Well Wishes

Congratulations! You have engaged in a lengthy and focused process. We hope that this *process* of Reiki and relaxation has proven to be an avenue leading to the release of tension. Perhaps you have come to see stress in new ways as you expanded your powers of perception. In the Reiki and relaxation process heightened awareness of self, and also the underlying, multidimensional, complex patterns of self within a whole system unfolds.

The 21-Day Reiki and Relaxation Process can be a starting point for a renewal of commitment to healthful attitudes—a renewal of the elimination of toxic substances and emotions from your universe of discourse. Perhaps during this 21-day journey you have found the ongoing process to be a valuable reconnecting device, always available even in your busiest moments, and an opportunity to tap into your highest wisdom. We hope so! Indeed, integrating such a process into your everyday life may bring you great comfort, on many levels.

We hope you have found that the *21-Day Process* has been helpful towards paying attention to your intuitive feelings (through focusing intent and journaling), and then responding to these feelings. We imagine that you have seen that the possibilities are limitless –the possibilities of the harmonious, coherent state which deep relaxation encourages. As you become a student of self, perhaps coming to new perspectives through the *21-Day Process Program*, will lead you to ask yourself as Dr. Usui himself once did.

Many blessings on your journey!

Appendices

APPENDIX A: MAKING CONTACT

*7*akata, the Initial Contact

Reiki, *The Usui System of Natural Healing*, was introduced to the West by Hawayo Takata. She was the first contact and teacher. Because of her efforts there are now hundreds of organizations and hundreds of thousands of Reiki practitioners.

One December day in 1980, Hawayo Takata made her transition, leaving behind a legacy, many students, and twenty-two teachers of Reiki. She had spent almost four decades sharing her wisdom. Her students had learned to treat Reiki with the respect it deserves. Her interest, as had been that of her teacher, Hayashi, and his teacher, Usui, was in helping people to awaken to their own special place in the universe. With this realization, she said, comes healing—on many levels.

Hawayo Takata was born on Christmas Eve in Kauai, Hawaii where she grew up, was married and widowed at an early age. This was the place she called home. She found Reiki in the way so many of its practitioners have—by fortuitous detours and happy twists of fate.

*M*ore Contacts

The Reiki Alliance
P. O. Box 41
Cataldo, ID 83810, USA
Phone: 1/208/682-3535

International Association of Reiki
Lesni 14
46001 Liberec 1
Czech Republic

Reiki Outreach International
P. O. Box 609
Fair Oaks, California 95628
Fax 916/863-6464

www.onedegreebeyond.com
for more organizations

Contacting a Reiki Master

The Initial Interview	Questions to Ask Yourself
❑ Tell me a little bit about yourself, and your background, and how you became a Reiki Master.	❑ Does this person seem sincere and dedicated?
❑ Tell me a little bit about *The Usui System of Reiki.*	❑ Was this person willing to spend at least half an hour talking and sharing with me?
❑ How long have you been involved in Reiki? Did it take you a long time to become a Reiki Master? What is your lineage?	❑ Did this person say "I" often, and in a controlling way, and answer from Ego?
	❑ Did this person seem mature?
❑ I've heard that Reiki can be effective in stress management. Is that true? Are there any other ways that Reiki can help me?	❑ Was there a definite spark of enthusiasm when Usui was discussed? What kind of depth and bond to *The Usui System* did you notice?
❑ How do you view your role in a Reiki Session?	❑ Did this Reiki Master display mastery by being able to answer the question "When can you speak to your self, from the center of the Universe?"
❑ Do you aim Reiki? Or how do you "get"it?	
❑ Who *does* the Reiki?	❑ Did you like this person?
❑ How did you come to teach Reiki? Are you a member of an organization? Are you certified to do hands-on work?	❑ Does this person seem to be someone you could respect?
	❑ Would *you* want to know this person over a long period of time?
❑ Do you have any long term students?	❑ What did *you* learn from your conversation?
❑ When can you speak to yourself from the center of the universe?	

APPENDIX B: COMPLEMENTARY SYSTEMS

Conscious Breathing

Lie down on your back. Make sure you are comfortable and on a comfortable surface. Your legs should be stretched out... your feet about a foot apart. Let your arms rest at your sides. Breathe very slowly, and become *aware* of your breathing.

Visualize, as you inhale, a scale filling with soft mountain air, refreshing you, then tipping, slowly releasing, in a slow out-breath, releasing tension as you let go of each breath.... Take long, slow, breaths... in and out... all the way to the last of each... pause after you exhale. Wait until your body nudges you to inhale. When that happens, consciously take a long, peaceful, *slow*, in-breath. (This process may take a few seconds or fifteen or thirty seconds....)

Don't hold your breath, but just let it gently slide into the next in/out, as you visualize the scale balancing, moving slowly in rhythm with your breathing. Allow your eyes to close as you focus on your breathing, now very deep and regular... balancing back and forth from way down to way up as you continue visualizing the scale. Breathe in through your nose. *Slowly*. Breathe out through your mouth. *Gently*.

Relax your body and let all the aches, pains, pressures float away with each exhale. Each breath you inhale brings with it peace and comfort as you breathe in the restful energy that is about you.

APPENDIX C: RESOURCES

Suggested Reading

Barber, Ph.D, Theodore Xenophon, *The Human Nature of Birds*, St. Martins Press, New York, NY, 1993.

Barnett, Libby and Chambers, Maggie, *Reiki, Energy Medicine*, Healing Arts Press, Rochester, VT, 1996.

Benson, Herbert, M.D., *The Relaxation Response*, Berkley Press, New York, NY, 1987.

Bohm, David, *Unfolding Meaning,* ARK Paperbacks, Rutledge, London, 1994.

Bohm, David, *Wholeness & the Implicate Order,* Rutledge, London, 1983.

Bohm, David and Hiley, Basil J., *The Undivided Universe,* Rutledge, London, 1994.

Brennan, Barbara Ann, *Hands of Light,* Bantam Books, New York, NY, 1979.

Briggs, John, and Peat, David, *Turbulent Mirror: An Illustrated Guide to Chaos, Theory, and the Science of Wholeness*, Harper Collins, New York, N.Y., 1990.

Clarke, C.J.S., *Reality Through the Looking Glass*, Floris Books, Edinburgh, Great Britain, 1966.

Cohen, Michael J., *Reconnecting with Nature*, Ecopress, Corvallis, OR, 1997.

Davies, Paul, *The Cosmic Blueprint*, Simon & Schuster, New York, NY, 1988.

Diamond, John, M.D., *Life Energy*, Paragon House, New York, NY, 1990.

Dossey, Larry, M.D., *Space, Time and Medicine*, Shambala Publications, Inc., Boston, MA., 1982.

Dossey, Larry, M.D., *Meaning and Medicine,* Bantam Books, New York, NY, 1991.

Ford, Clyde, *Where Healing Waters Meet*, Station Hill Press, Barrytown, NY, 1989.

Fox, Matthew, *The Reinvention of Work*, Harper-Collins, New York, NY, 1994.

Fox, Matthew and Rupert Sheldrake, *Natural Grace*, Doubleday Publishers, New York, NY, 1996.

Fox, Matthew and Rupert Sheldrake, *The Physics of Angels*, Harper-Collins, New York, NY, 1996.

Fox, Matthew, *Original Blessing*, Bear & Co., Santa Fe, NM, 1983.

Gerber, Richard, M.D., *Vibrational Medicine*, Bear & Co., Inc., Santa Fe, NM, 1988.

Gleisner, Earlene F., R.N., *Reiki in Everyday Living*, White Feather Press, Laytonville, CA, 1992.

Griffin, David Ray, *The Reenchantment of Science*, Postmodern Proposals, State University of New York Press, Albany, NY, 1988.

Grof, Stanislav, *Beyond the Brain*, State University of New York Press, Albany, NY, 1985.

Hall, Mari, *Practical Reiki*, Thorsons, London, 1997.

Hendricks, Gay, Ph.D., *Conscious Breathing*, Bantam Books, New York, NY, 1995.

Horan, Paula, Ph.D., *Empowerment Through Reiki*, Lotus Light Publications, Wilmot, WI, 1989.

Houston, Jean, *Godseed, The Journey of Christ*, Quest Books, Wheaton, IL., 1992.

Kabat-Zinn, Jon, Ph.D., *Wherever You Go, There you Are*, Hyperion, New York, NY, 1990.

Kabat-Zinn, Jon, Ph.D., *Full Catastrophe Living, Using the Wisdom of Your Body and Mind to Face Stress, Pain, and Illness*, Dell Publishing, New York, NY, 1990.

Krishnamurti, J. and Bohm, David, *The Ending of Time*, Harper-Collins, San Francisco, CA 1985.

Mackenzie, Donald A., *Myths of Japan*, Gramercy Books, New York, NY, 1994.

Marrett, Barbara, *Mahina Tiare*, Pacific International Publishing Co., Friday Harbor, WA., 1993.

McColman, Carl, *Spirituality, Where Body and Soul Encounter the Sacred*, North Star Publications, Georgetown, MA, 1997

Mitchell, Paul David, *The Usui System of Natural Healing*, The Reiki Alliance, Coeur d'Alene, ID, 1985.

Montagu, Ashley, *Touching, The Human Significance of the Skin*, Harper and Row Publishers, New York, NY, 1986.

Myss, Caroline, Ph.D., *Anatomy of the Spirit*, Crown, New York, NY, 1996.

Myss, Caroline, Ph.D., *Why People Don't Heal and How They Can*, Harmony Books, New York, NY, 1997.

Peat, F. David, *Lighting the Seventh Fire*, Carol Publishing Group, New York, NY, 1994.

Peat, F. David, *Infinite Potential, the Life and Times of David Bohm,* Addison-Wesley, Reading, MA, 1997.

Pribam, Karl, *Languages of the Brain*, Wadsworth Publishing, Monterey, CA, 1977.

Prigogine, Ilya, *The End of Certainty*, The Free Press, Monterey, CA, 1977.

Russell, Peter, *The White Hole in Time*, Harper San Francisco, New York, NY, 1992.

Sardello, Robert, *Facing the World With Soul*, Continuum Publishers Group, New York, N.Y., 1994.

Shealy, Norman, M.D., Ph.D., and Myss, Caroline, *The Creation of Health*, Stillpoint Publishing, Walpole, NH, 1993.

Sheldrake, Rupert, *A New Science of Life,* Blond & Briggs, London, 1981.

Sogyal, Rinpoche, The Tibetan Book of Living and Dying, Harper San Francisco, San Francisco, CA., 1994.

Swimme, Brian, *The Universe is a Green Dragon*, Bear and Co., Inc., Santa Fe, NM, 1985.

Swimme, Brian, *The Hidden Heart of the Cosmos*, Orbis Books, New York, NY, 1996.

Swimme, Brian and Berry, Thomas, *The Universe Story*, Harper-Collins Publishers, New York, NY, 1992.

Talbot, Michael, *The Holographic Universe*, Harper Collins, New York, NY, 1991.

Teilhard de Chardin, Pierre, *The Future of Man*, Harper & Row, New York, NY, 1959.

Teilhard de Chardin, Pierre, *The Heart of Matter,* Harcourt, Brace, Javonovich Publishers, New York, NY, 1959.

Tiller, William, "Energy Fields and the Human Body," *Frontiers of Consciousness*, edited by J. White. Avon Books, New York, NY, 1974.

Twan, Wanja, *In the Light of a Distant Star*, Morning Star Productions, Vancouver, B.C., Canada

Weil, Andrew, M.D., *Spontaneous Healing*, Alfred A. Knopf, Inc., New York, NY, 1995.

Weiss, Brian L., M.D., *Through Time into Healing*, Fireside Books, Simon & Shuster, New York, NY, 1992.

Wilber, Ken, *A Brief History of Everything*, Shambhala, Boston, 1996.

Zukav, Gary, *The Dancing WuLi Masters,* William Morrow & Co., New York, NY, 1979.

Suggested "Surfing"

One Degree Beyond... (*and its links*)
http://www.onedegreebeyond.com
Project NatureConnect
http://www.pacificrim.net/nature/.www.html
Union of Concerned Scientists
http://www.uscusa.org/
New and Alternative Theories of Physics
http://www.weburbia.com/pg/theories.htm
http://www.weburbia.demon.co.uk/pg/theories.htm
ISSSEEM (Studies of Subtle Energy)
http://vitalenergy.com/issseem
Subtle Energy Research and Physical Health
http://www.vitalenergy.com/seraph
Complementary and Alternative Medicine Program at Stanford
http://scrdp.standord.edu/camps.html
Center for Alternative Medicine Research/Asthma
http://www-camra.vedavis.edu/
Reference Links - Energy Medicine, Ki Work and More
http://www.enteract.com/-being/
Four Noble Truths
http://home.earthlink.net/-srame/index.html
American Holistic Nurses' Association
http://www.ahna.org/Latest in Neutrino Research Information
Institute of HeartMath
http://www.heartmath.org
Institute of Noetic Sciences
http://www.noetic.org/

£nergy Medicine Research Articles and Abstracts

Becker, Robert O., M.D., "Evidence for a Primitive DC Electrical Analog System Controlling Brain Function," *ISSSEEM Journal,* Vol. 2, No. 1, 1991.

Benor, Daniel J., M.D., "Lessons from Spiritual Healing Research and Practice," *ISSSEEM Journal,* Vol. 3, No. 1, 1992.

Braud, William G. Ph.D., and Schlitz, Marilyn J., M.A., "Consciousness Interactions with Remote Biological Systems: Anomalous Intentionality Effects," *ISSSEEM Journal,* Vol. 2, No. 1, 1991.

Fahrion, Steven L., Ph.D., Wirkus, Mietek, and Pooley, Patricia, "EEG Amplitude, Brain Mapping, and Synchrony in and Between a Bioenergy Practitioner and Client Healing," *ISSSEEM Journal,* Vol. 2, No. 1, 1992.

Gough, W.C., and Shacklett, Robert, "The Science of Connectiveness, part 1: Modeling a Greater Unity," *ISSSEEM Journal*, Vol. 4, No. 1, 1993.

Matzke, D., "Prediction: Future Electronic Systems will be Disrupted Due to Consciousness," *Toward a Science of Consciousness*, MIT Press, 1994.

Peat, F. David, Ph.D., "Towards a Process Theory of Healing: Energy, Activity and Global Form," *ISSSEEM Journal*, Vol 3., No. 2, 1992.

Radin, Dean I., Ph.D., "Beyond Belief: Exploring Interactions Among Mind, Body and Environment," *ISSSEEM Journal*, Vol 2, No. 3, 1991.

Redner, Robin, Ph.D., Briner, Barbara, D.O., and Snellman, Lynn, M.S., "Effects of a Bioenergy Healing Technique on Chronic Pain," *ISSSEEM Journal*, Vol. 2, No. 3, 1991.

Schwartz, Gary E., Ph.D., Russek, Linda G., Ph.D., and Beltran, Justin, "Interpersonal Hand-Energy Registration; Evidence of Implicit Performance and Perception," *ISSSEEM Journal,* Vol. 6, No. 3, 1995.

Thompson, Richard, "Numerical Analysis and Theoretical Modelling of Causal Effects of Conscious Intention," *ISSSEEM Journal*, Vol. 2, No. 1, 1991.

W. Harman, "Toward a Science of Consciousness: Addressing Two Central Questions," *Toward a Science of Consciousness*, MIT Press, 1994.

INDEX

About the Author

Janeanne Narrin, M.A., C.S.W., whose background is in industrial psychology and business (her career spans many years in management consulting), is a master teacher in *The Usui System of Reiki*. Her interest in right livelihood and in the effects of stress on personnel in the workplace prompted her to actively seek out innovative stress release techniques. While on this search, she discovered Reiki, a methodology she describes as wedding contemporary scientific knowledge with age-old insight.

"It's a practice that encourages its practitioners to empower themselves," she says. "Reiki's something you access to relieve and dissolve stress. It also enlivens, has restorative potential, and encourages self-actualization, a social conscience, and optimism." When her schedule doesn't find her on the seminar trail, Narrin continues to pursue her interests in writing, painting, poetry, and photography.

To receive information about current workshops and trainings offered, please contact her organizer at the following address:

12345 Lake City Way, N.E.
Suite 204
Seattle, WA. 98125

 *Little White Buffalo Publishing Cottage*
Synthesizing knowledge for the global good, and
conveying a vision of hope.

Forthcoming Titles:

Author: Wind-in-the-Feather (Poet of *One Degree Beyond*)
Title: *Quantum Breeze: Meditations in Postmodern Time*

Author: Janeanne Narrin
Title: *Energy Medicine in Cyberspace*

Author: David A. Bishop
Title: *Sacred Spaces: Notes from the Margin*

Little White Buffalo Publishing Cottage
Synthesizing knowledge for the global good, and
conveying a vision of hope.

We invite you to share this book with your library, family and friends.

Visit your local bookseller for browsing, personal selection and that special atmosphere found only in a bookstore.

Find us online:
http://www.barnesandnoble.com
http://www.littlewhitebuffalo.com
http://www.Amazon.com

Individual orders: send check or money order to:
LWBPC 12345 Lake City Way, N.E., Suite 204, Seattle, WA 98125
($18.95 + $4.00 for shipping and handling)

Credit card orders at our toll free ordering line: 1•800•247•6553

Thank you for sharing our books and enlivening hearts and minds!

Volume discounts are available.